ON RUSSIAN MUSIC

GLINKA

On Russian Music

GERALD ABRAHAM

faber and faber

To J.A. Westrup,
who stood godfather to many of these studies

This edition first published in 2013
by Faber and Faber Ltd
Bloomsbury House, 74–77 Great Russell Street
London WC1B 3DA

Printed by Books on Demand GmbH, Norderstedt

All rights reserved
© Gerald Abraham, 1939

The right of Gerald Abraham to be identified
as author of this work has been asserted in accordance
with Section 77 of the Copyright, Designs and Patents Act 1988

This book is sold subject to the condition that it shall not, by way of
trade or otherwise, be lent, resold, hired out or otherwise circulated
without the publisher's prior consent in any form of binding or cover other than
that in which it is published and without a similar condition including this
condition being imposed on the subsequent purchaser

A CIP record for this book is available from the British Library

ISBN 978–0–571–30727–2

PREFACE

The success of my collection of "Studies in Russian Music" encourages me to issue this supplementary, or rather complementary, volume. In the earlier book Glinka and Balakirev were dismissed with a chapter apiece; here I have devoted separate studies to Glinka's two operas, to Balakirev's Symphonies, to his Piano Sonata and to his "King Lear" music. The Borodin and Dargomïzhsky chapters are supplementary in the same way, the essay on the history of "Prince Igor" providing an (I hope) illuminating pendant to the analysis of its musical texture in the earlier book, while the chapters on "Mlada" and "Tsar Saltan" complete the series of studies of Rimsky-Korsakov's really important operas. The rest of the book deals mainly with various general aspects of Russian music, though I have still limited myself to the period 1836-1910.

Most of these essays have appeared in slightly different forms in "Music and Letters," "Musical Opinion," "The Musical Times," "The Monthly Musical Record," "The Radio Times," "The Sackbut" and "The Contemporary Review," and I offer my grateful thanks to the respective editors for permission to reprint them.

G. A.

CONTENTS.

		PAGE
I.	"A Life for the Tsar"	1
II.	"Ruslan and Lyudmila"	20
III.	Glinka, Dargomïzhsky and "The Rusalka"	43
IV.	Dargomïzhsky's Orchestral Pieces	52
V.	The Whole-Tone Scale in Russian Music	62
VI.	Oriental Elements in Russian Music	72
VII.	Liszt's Influence on the "Mighty Handful"	81
VIII.	The Collective "Mlada"	91
IX.	Rimsky-Korsakov's "Mlada"	113
X.	"Tsar Saltan"	122
XI.	New Light on Old Friends. (a) The Programme of "Scheherazade." (b) The Programme of the "Pathétique" Symphony	138
XII.	The History of "Prince Igor"	147
XIII.	Borodin's Songs	169
XIV.	Balakirev's Symphonies	179
XV.	Balakirev's Music to "King Lear"	193
XVI.	Balakirev's Piano Sonata	205
XVII.	"The Fair of Sorochintsy" and Cherepnin's Completion of It	216
XVIII.	"Eugene Onegin" and Tchaïkovsky's Marriage	225
XIX.	Glazunov: The End of an Episode	234
XX.	Some Psychological Peculiarities of Russian Creative Artists	243
XXI.	The Evolution of Russian Harmony	255
	Index	275

ON RUSSIAN MUSIC

I.—"A LIFE FOR THE TSAR."

Everyone who knows anything at all about Russian music "knows" that Glinka's "Life for the Tsar" was "the first Russian opera." Like a good many other well-known facts of musical history, it happens to be not quite correct. "A Life for the Tsar" was neither the first opera composed on a Russian subject or to a Russian text, the first opera by a Russian composer, nor (in the opinion of the present writer) the opera that really laid the foundation-stone of modern Russian music. True, it happens to be the first of the only two operas written by the first Russian composer of any importance; but, even so, it is not—historically considered—a beginning of anything. Rather it is an end, a summing-up, the best and almost the last blossom produced by a rather sickly plant. The true foundation stone of Russian opera, as the world knows it, was the work that followed "A Life for the Tsar"—"Ruslan and Lyudmila." Still, "A Life for the Tsar" contains too much living music and enjoys too great a history-book reputation to be curtly dismissed as a mere relic of an earlier age. Without knowing it, one cannot properly recognise the enormous importance, the daring of "Ruslan." And, in turn, one cannot truly appreciate "A Life for the Tsar" without at least a rough idea of its predecessors.

The first opera written to a Russian text was "Cephalos and Procris," by Francesco Araja, the Empress Elizabeth's *maestro di cappella*. It was performed on February 27-March 11, 1755, at the Court Theatre, Petersburg, by an all-Russian cast—also an innovation. The next year we hear of another work that has been claimed as "the first opera by a Russian composer." This was the operetta "Tanyusha," of which the music is said to have been "arranged" by Fyodor Volkov. But Volkov was not a composer but an actor, the "first Court actor" of the Imperial Russian Theatre which was established the same year (1756). As for "Tanyusha," even the libretto has disappeared; we know nothing at all about it. The first opera definitely composed by a Russian was Fomin's "Anyuta" (first performance: August 26-September 7, 1772), but even of this only the libretto survives. And the next operas by Russian musicians of which we hear were settings of Italian texts, *written and produced in Italy:* Maxim Berezovsky's "Demofonte" (Leghorn, 1773), and Bortnyansky's "Creonte" (Venice, 1776).

That is symptomatic. Of the five native composers who were writing Russian operas in the seventies and eighties of the eighteenth century—Fomin (1741-1800), Matinsky (died 1820), Berezovsky (1745-77), Bortnyansky (1751-1825), and Pashkevich (?-?)—the first four all studied in Italy. Another symptom: Fomin and Matinsky* were both liberated serfs and both were at first purely self-taught musicians. It seems probable, though we do not know for certain, that they too, like Berezovsky and Bortnyansky, began their careers as operatic composers in Italy. As for the court composer, Pashkevich, if he never studied in Italy, he produced several works in collaboration with the foreign composers in favour at the Court of Catherine the Great (who was herself their librettist)—with Sarti, Carlo Canobbio, and Vincente Martin y Soler.

These composers, even the foreigners, appreciated the flavour of the national folk-music more than might have been expected. Fomin used folk-tunes, or good imitations of them, in several of his

---

* Whom one English writer on Russian music has taken to be an opera by Fomin!

operas. Findeisen* considers this passage from the overture to his best work, "The Miller" (1781), which kept the stage for more than seventy years, "more or less Russian in character":—

The chief theme of the overture to Matinsky's "Bazaar at St. Petersburg" (1779):—

is much more definitely Russian; it is even a faint anticipation of Olga's theme in Rimsky-Korsakov's "Pskovityanka." And Canobbio in the Prelude to Act III of "The Early Reign of Oleg" (1790; in collaboration with Pashkevich and Sarti) introduces the famous "Kamarinskaya," the indecent *tsigane* dance appearing under a mask of propriety in the disguise of a thoroughly respectable minuet:—

---

* In his study of "The Earliest Russian Operas," translated by Calvocoressi in "The Musical Quarterly," July, 1933.

"A Life for the Tsar."

But these were only oases in the desert of Italian or quasi-Italian music produced at the Imperial Court. Some of the foreign Court composers—e.g., Paesiello, never even attempted to set Russian texts; others, such as the Neapolitan, Catterino Cavos (1776-1840), definitely Russianised themselves, wrote operas based on Russian legends and episodes from Russian history, and tried to catch the inflections of popular melody. Cavos actually anticipated the subject of "A Life for the Tsar" in his "Ivan Susanin" (1815). And the native amateur strain lived on in figures like Verstovsky (1799-1862), Alyabiev (1787-1851), and the brothers Titov (Alexey, 1769-1827, and Sergey, born 1770). Thus Russian opera for more than half-a-century was composed by through-and-through Italians, by superficially Russianised Italians, by Italian trained Russians, and by Russian amateurs who took this Italo-Russian music as their model. Of these the Italians were at least competent technicians, but the Russians—even those who had studied abroad—seem to have been as weak in technique as in inspiration. Apart from its historical interest, their collective output (as far as one can judge from the specimens obtainable) is an insipid pot-pourri of the musical platitudes of the day, faintly flavoured with native condiments.

Nevertheless, it is to this genre that "A Life for the Tsar" belongs. Its composer, too, was a wealthy dilettante who had studied only desultorily, who had just spent a three years' holiday in Italy, and who was full of admiration for the Italian opera of his day—writing rondos "on a theme from 'Montecchi e Capuletti,'" serenades "on themes from 'Anna Bolena,'" and similar artistic atrocities. And he wrote his first opera in this Russian-flavoured Italian idiom.* But with these differences: that the native flavouring was stronger and that he himself had a genuine creative gift denied to his predecessors.

Even before he left Italy in 1833, at the age of twenty-nine, Glinka had seen that "the Italian *sentimento brilliante* is the result of an organism happily developed under the beneficent influence of southern sunshine. We dwellers in the North feel differently: impressions either leave us altogether untouched or penetrate deeply into the soul—with us it is a matter of either frantic merriment or bitter tears. With us, love is always linked with sadness." He had tried to make an Italian of himself, but had failed. "Homesickness gradually led me to the idea of writing in Russian." And on his leisurely way home from Italy he composed, à

---

* Cui's dictum that "in the whole of the opera there is hardly a single musical phrase having closer affinity with the music of Western Europe than with the Slavs" is a gross exaggeration. It is unfortunate that Cui's association with the "mighty handful" has armed him with apparent authority as a critic, and that his book, "La Musique en Russie," has laid the foundation of so many Western judgments of Russian music. Cui was no better critic than he was composer. The majority of his judgments, on friend and foe alike, are very wide of the mark.

propos of nothing in particular, several themes which he was afterwards able to use in his first opera: in Vienna the clarinet theme of the *Krakoviak*, in Berlin (where he studied with Siegfried Dehn for four or five months) the melody of Vanya's song at the beginning of Act III (i.e., the second Allegro subject of the Overture), and the theme of the finale of the same act (i.e., the *first* subject of the Allegro of the Overture).

From Berlin he wrote in January, 1834: "I have a scheme in my head, an idea .... Perhaps this isn't the moment to make a complete confession; perhaps if I told you everything I should be afraid of detecting signs of incredulity in your face. And yet I ought to warn you that you will find me somewhat changed; I'm sure you'll be astonished to find much more in me than you could have believed at the time when I was living in Petersburg. Must I tell you? Well, I fancy that I, even I, have the ability to give our stage a work on a large scale. It won't be a masterpiece, as I am the first to admit, but all the same it won't be so bad! What do you say to this? The main thing is to choose the subject well. It will be absolutely national in every respect. And not only the subject but the music; I want my fellow-countrymen to feel absolutely at home in it, and I *don't* want to be considered abroad as a vainglorious jay decked out in borrowed plumage." Six months later he had still not found a suitable libretto. "But the idea of 'Marina

Grove'* kept revolving in my head, and I played on the piano several fragments of scenes which afterwards partly served me for 'A Life for the Tsar.'"

Curiously enough, it was the author of "Marina Grove" himself, poet, critic and former tutor to the Tsarevich, who set him on the right track. I give the story as Glinka himself tells it in his Memoirs:

"When I avowed my wish to write a Russian opera, Zhukovsky [who was anxious to create an artistic nimbus about the throne] sincerely approved my intention, and suggested to me the subject of 'Ivan Susanin.'† The scene in the forest [with the Poles in Act IV] deeply impressed itself on my imagination. I found in it much that was original and typically Russian. Zhukovsky wanted to write the words himself, and as a specimen wrote some lines used for the trio with chorus in the Epilogue. His affairs prevented his carrying out his intention, so he put me in touch with Baron Rosen, an industrious German man of letters, who was at

---

* A sentimental story by Zhukovsky, which was enjoying considerable popularity at that time.

† The very simple plot is based on an historical incident of doubtful authenticity. A peasant, Susanin, is said to have saved the life of the young Tsar Michael (about 1612-13) at the cost of his own by leading a body of Polish troops into a marshy forest from which they were unable to escape. Susanin's daughter, Antonida, and a young peasant, Bogdan Sobinin, provide the "love interest" of the opera; his adopted son, Vanya, is the principal contralto rôle.

that time secretary to H.I.H. the Tsarevich. My imagination, however, forestalled the industrious German: as if by magic both the plan of the whole opera and the idea of the antithesis of Russian and Polish music, as well as many of the themes and even details of the working-out—all this flashed into my head at one stroke.* I began to work, and from the wrong end; for I began with the part that others write last—the overture, which I wrote for piano four hands, with indications of the scoring. In the published version for four hands, the Overture is preserved just as I wrote it then, except the Adagio, which I afterwards changed. Themes for different parts of the opera, often with indications of contrapuntal treatment, were written down in notebooks as I invented them. . . . During the spring—i.e., in March and April, 1835—Rosen prepared the libretto of Acts I and II according to my plan. This gave him more than a little trouble, for a great part, not only of the themes but of the working-out of the numbers, was already done; and he had to fit the words to the music, which sometimes demanded the strangest metres. But Rosen was a splendid fellow at this: you only had to ask

---

* According to his friend, Prince Odoevsky, however, "Glinka's first idea was to write not an opera, but something in the way of a picture, as he said, or scenic oratorio. As far as I can remember he wanted to confine himself to *only three tableaux:* the village scene, the Polish scene, and the final triumph." But the first draft of the first three acts has been preserved, and it agrees fairly closely with the final scenario.

for so many lines in such-and-such a metre. It was all the same to him: you came back next day, and there they were."

The composer was on the eve of his marriage, and he tells us that "the thought of the well-known Trio" in Act I "was the consequence of my insane love: a minute without my *fiancée* seemed to me intolerable, and I really felt the lover's impatience expressed in the Adagio or Andante, 'Do not make us suffer, father,' which I had written in the country during the summer." He took the libretto of the first two acts with him on his honeymoon:—

"And I remember that somewhere beyond Novgorod I composed the 'Bridal Chorus' in 5-4 time in the carriage. The details of our life in the country have escaped my memory: I only know that I worked diligently. Every morning I sat at the table of the big, cheerful drawing-room in our house at Novospasskoe. It was our favourite room: sisters, mother, wife—in fact, the whole family—swarmed there, and the more noisily they laughed and chattered the quicker went my work. The weather was lovely, and I often worked with the door open into the garden, drinking in the pure fragrant air. I first wrote the Trio in 2-4 time and in A minor, but reflected that I had already got a lot of duple time in the first act—viz., the Introduction, Antonida's aria, and Susanin's recitative; so rewrote the melody in 6-8 and in B flat minor, which far better expressed the languor of love."

It was much the same when the newly married pair returned to St. Petersburg:—

"Work went well. Every morning I sat at the table and wrote half-a-dozen or so pages of score. .... The scene of Susanin in the forest with the Poles was written during the winter. I frequently read the whole of this scene aloud before I began the composition, and so vividly imagined myself in the position of my hero that my hair stood on end and I felt frozen with fear."

Even before it was finished, the new opera was tried out piecemeal at private houses during the winter. For instance, the first act was given at Prince Yusupov's, with his rather mediocre private orchestra. Some of the artists of the Imperial Opera (among them the famous bass, Petrov, and his wife) took part; and at another such rehearsal at Count Vielhorsky's, A. M. Gedeonov, the director of the Imperial theatres, was present. Everybody was ready with advice. Vielhorsky made two suggestions:—

"The Introduction had no coda, and on his advice I added one. In No. 3, in the scene with Susanin (the chief theme of which is taken from a Russian song I heard near the town of Luga) before the arrival of the bridegroom, there was no chorus on the stage, but only behind the scenes. The Count advised me to add the chorus on the stage *crescendo* and end it *ff*, which I did successfully, and the appearance of the bridegroom [Sobinin] was made incomparably more brilliant. In the course of the work, I was not a little indebted to the advice of Prince Odoevsky, and somewhat to that of Charles Mayer [Glinka's old piano teacher]. Odoevsky was extraordinary pleased with the theme I had taken from the Luga coachman's song:—

"He advised me to bring in a reminiscence of this scene (with which Susanin's part opens) in the last scene in the forest with the Poles. I managed to do this: at the words 'Here I have brought you —to weariness, fear, death and the judgment of God!' occurs a progression based on a fragment from the theme given me by the coachman. In the composition of the beginning of Susanin's replies, I had in mind our well-known robbers' song, 'Down by Mother Volga,' using its beginning in doubled time as an accompaniment figure*:

---

* In these quotations I have used a manuscript version made by an anonymous translator for the British National Opera Company.

"I sometimes consulted Charles Mayer on the scoring, particularly in *ff*. I remember also that he suggested an effective accompaniment figure in the mazurka [the rhythmic pedal on horn, oboe, etc.].

"At the end of the summer, I wrote the trio with chorus, 'Ah, not to me, poor wretched one,' in the Epilogue, inspired by the talent of Madame Vorobieva [Petrov's wife, the celebrated contralto, who created the rôle of Vanya in this opera; she died as recently as 1901]. I wrote this trio (from which I constructed the Adagio of the Overture) in an hour of merriment. I remember, as if it were now, that there were fifteen of us fellows at Kukolnik's flat, and that I wrote, or more correctly *composed*, this touching scene amid the noise and conversation of my carousing friends."*

The official rehearsals had begun before this, under the direction of that same Neapolitan, Cavos, who had composed an opera on the same subject twenty years before, and who, from first to last, showed a commendable freedom from jealousy. The Emperor himself appeared at one of the rehearsals and not only expressed his approval but was graciously pleased to accept the dedication of the opera. It was forthwith re-named "A Life for the Tsar." (Since the Revolution, it has discreetly

---

* In August, 1837, at Petrov's request, Glinka added a new scene, No. 19, for Vanya. It replaces No. 18. The words were written by Kukolnik, and Glinka composed the whole scene in one day.

reverted to its original title, "Ivan Susanin," but it is still frequently performed.) The whole of the Imperial family were present at the first performance (November 27-December 9, 1836); the composer was summoned to the Imperial box, and rewarded a few days later with a four thousand ruble ring. Glinka found himself recognised as "the first composer in Russia." It became a patriotic duty to attend his opera; the "Slavsya" was adopted as a sort of secondary national anthem; and "A Life for the Tsar" was thus given a factitious importance which inflated its artistic value, considerable as that is.

To what does this "artistic value" really amount? The opera is so unequal that it is difficult to appraise it as a whole. The very first page of the first act is typical. A male chorus, led by a soloist in true Russian folk-song style, sings an unaccompanied *quasi*-folk-song amateurishly harmonised:—

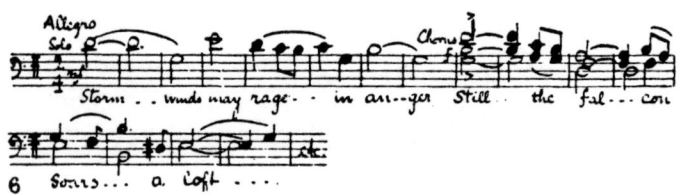

each stanza being rounded off by a snatch of very banal orchestral ritornello. The music is a little more genuinely Russian in flavour than the work of

Fomin and Matinsky; though not much. But this chorus, very square in construction though it is, improves as it goes on. A women's chorus enters with a fresh theme, and the two subjects are combined in naïve but very effective counterpoint. There are finer and more truly national things in the score than this: the unison chorus accompanying Sobinin's arrival, with its racy pizzicato accompaniment (anticipating the Scherzo of Tchaïkovsky's Fourth Symphony) in imitation of balalaikas:—

and the lovely Bridal Chorus in Act III :—

But, on the whole, the national flavour is seldom stronger than in Ex. 6, and frequently a great deal weaker. The fault, as with all the dilettante school, is more harmonic than melodic; even when Glinka writes a modal melody, as he not infrequently does, he accompanies it diatonically. Again and again a bit of melodic line, needing only the merest suspicion of characteristic harmonic spice (such as the G sharp in bar 3 of Ex. 8) to bring out its essential Russian flavour, is reduced to insipidity by the most banal harmonisation. Nothing could be more striking than the contrast between the almost unrelieved harmonic tameness of "A Life for the Tsar" and the harmonic daring of "Ruslan."

But, in one respect, other than purely musical quality, Glinka's first opera does stand far in advance not only of all earlier Russian operas, but of all contemporary (and even many later) operas whatsoever. As Serov and others have proudly pointed out, Glinka was a pioneer in the use of the leitmotive—or rather of theme-quotation for dramatic purposes. Such quotation is far more extensive in "A Life for the Tsar" than in anything by Weber or any other pre-Wagnerian composer. The very first phrase of the opera (Ex. 6) is quoted in Act III, when Susanin fearlessly bares his breast to the Poles and cries that he does not fear to die for his Tsar and for Russia; and the same theme is effectively woven into the entr'acte before the Epilogue, in contrast with the mazurka theme symbolising the Poles.

Glinka's own account of the use of Susanin's first

"A Life for the Tsar."

song again in his last scene has already been quoted. But nearly all the dramatic value of Susanin's last monologue as he awaits the dawn—a fine and moving passage—depends on its calling up of one theme after another, half-a-dozen of them, heard earlier in the opera and firmly associated with Antonida, Sobinin and Vanya. The theme of the massive "Slavsya" chorus of the Epilogue, glorifying the Tsar, is several times subtly hinted at previously in the score; Susanin sings the opening phrase of it in his first scene with the Poles (Act III):—

As for the Poles themselves, they exist musically in nothing but leitmotives. We accept the polonaise and mazurka of Act II (the Polish festival) as pleasant, undistinguished ballet music, nothing more. But when the Poles break in, in Act III, we find that they bring the polonaise and mazurka themes with them as national emblems and have no musical existence apart from these emblems.

This naïve characterisation of the Poles by national dance-rhythms, which has irritated some critics by its crudity as much as it has won praise from others for its theatrical effectiveness, inevitably makes one think of "Boris" with its Polish act. The polonaise of "Boris" is not without a recollection of that in "A Life for the Tsar," though it must be admitted that the Polish acts of both works are by far their weakest parts.

But the prototype of many a better known number of later Russian opera may be found in this first work of Glinka's. The brisk, crisp overture obviously set the pattern for those of "Prince Igor" and "The Tsar's Bride." Antonida's cavatina, with voice (unaccompanied or very lightly accompanied) echoing long-drawn arabesque phrases on clarinet or flute, must have been the direct model for Konchakovna's cavatina in "Igor" and half-a-dozen similar songs in Rimsky-Korsakov's operas (e.g., Oxana's mirror aria in "Christmas Eve"), just as the modal chorus of peasants in Act III, with its charmingly transparent orchestral accompaniment, full of bright clear tints, is the prototype of a good many passages in Rimsky-Korsakov's opera scores.

The most curious of all the marks stamped on later and greater Russian works by "A Life for the Tsar" is of quite a different nature, however. It is an identity of a phrase, in a part of the work that one would hardly expect to have exercised much influence of any kind (the trio in Act I), with an extremely well-known theme in a Russian work that one hardly connects in one's mind with Glinka at all: Tchaïkovsky's Fifth Symphony. As far as I am aware, the coincidence has never been observed even by Russian critics. But it is undeniable that the motto-theme of the symphony is practically identical with Sobinin's phrase, "Do not turn to sorrow (the hour of our re-union)":—

We know from Tchaïkovsky's diary that he had been thinking much of "A Life for the Tsar" at the very time he began the Symphony (June, 1888), and the words suggest that the coincidence was due to no mere accident or trick of his memory. The melody is identical in intervals and (practically) in rhythm, though not in tonal function—it begins on the dominant instead of on the mediant—with the minor form of Tchaïkovsky's theme. And the harmonies are identical with Tchaïkovsky's harmonisation of the major form of his theme in the finale of the Symphony.

II.—"RUSLAN AND LYUDMILA."

If all the Russian music, other than folk-songs, written before Glinka's "Ruslan and Lyudmila" were wiped out of existence, the world would not be very much the poorer. There are some beautiful things in "A Life for the Tsar," but, as we have just seen, Glinka's first opera is of little more than historic interest. "Ruslan" is a different matter. Despite the dreamlike incoherence of its action, despite its occasional patches of weak and conventional music, it is a genuine masterpiece. "A Life for the Tsar" takes only a few timid steps into the "new world" of nineteenth century Russian music. "Ruslan" marches boldly into it.

"Two new elements contribute to the musical beauty of 'Ruslan and Lyudmila,'" says Calvocoressi.* "The archaism of the old Russian heroic style, introduced in music for the first time and

---

* "Glinka : biographie critique." Paris, 1911.

"*Ruslan and Lyudmila.*"

which was later to be exploited by Balakirev, Mussorgsky and Borodin in 'Russia,' 'Khovanshchina,' 'Prince Igor' and the B minor Symphony; and the orientalism which was to penetrate the whole of Russian music. A third, for which Glinka was no doubt indebted to Weber,* and which is of the highest importance, is the magical romanticism so favourable to the free development of the musical imagination."

This deepening and intensification of the national element in Glinka's music can hardly be attributed to the influence of the youthful poem of Pushkin's on which the opera is based. Writing of Pushkin's "Ruslan," D. S. Mirsky says† that "what is really most conspicuous in the poem is that bracing cold of eighteenth century frivolous sensuality which refuses to take life solemnly and uses everything to build up a romantic (if you like) but fantastic, unreal ballet-like decoration. The poetry of 'Ruslan and Lyudmila' is closely akin to the poetry of the classical ballet, and it is not irrelevant to compare it to the splendid ballets of Didelot, which were then the most popular show in Petersburg and of which Pushkin wrote a little later with such enthusiasm.

---

* Although Glinka had a poor opinion of Weber, even of "Der Freischütz." He complained to Liszt of Weber's "excessive use of the dominant seventh in root position." To which Liszt replied: "Vous êtes avec Weber comme deux rivaux, qui courtisez la même femme."

† "Pushkin." Routledge, 1926.

It was, in fact, before long turned into a ballet and was popular on the stage for many years in this form, until Glinka made it the libretto for his opera. On its appearance [in 1820] the poem was greeted by some and condemned by others for its romanticism and excess of 'national colour.' It is difficult now to understand this impression. Of course the style is distantly related to that of Ariosto, but it is permeated with the atmosphere of the eighteenth century and not very much more romantic than 'Zadig' or 'La Princesse de Babylone.' . . . The 'national' element is even less conspicuous. It amounts to a few names and a few very modified and 'frenchified' situations. . . . The names of Kiev and Vladimir [who in Glinka's opera is called Svetozar] were suggested by the old epic folk-songs published in 1804 (and again in 1818), but of the spirit of either romance or folk-epic there is nothing in Pushkin's poem. It is a highly elaborate and artistic toy. . . . There is no 'significance' or 'symbolism' behind the gallant adventures of 'Ruslan and Lyudmila.' It is just an agreeable poetic pageant."

There, of course, Mirsky is perfectly right. Nevertheless it is amusing to note that Dostoevsky with characteristic misplaced ingenuity contrived to read into Glinka's opera a symbolic meaning congenial to his Slavophile political views. His daughter Lyubov tells us* that when he took his children

---

* "Fyodor Dostoevsky: A Study." Heinemann, 1921.

to the opera "he always chose 'Ruslan and Lyudmila.' . . . My father seems to have wished to engrave the legend on our childish hearts. It is indeed very curious; it is a political allegory, prefiguring the destiny of the Slav nations. Lyudmila, the daughter of Prince Vladimir, represents the Western Slavs. Chernomor, an Oriental magician, a hideous dwarf with a long beard, who personifies Turkey, arrives at Kiev when a great festival is in progress, plunges everyone into a magic sleep, and carries off the fair Lyudmila to his castle. Two knights, Ruslan (Russia) and Farlaf (Austria), pursue the dwarf, and after many adventures arrive at Chernomor's castle," and so on. This fantastic interpretation conveniently overlooks the amiable oriental prince Ratmir. But it is hardly necessary to point out that the alleged symbolism throws light on nothing but Dostoevsky's mind and only a confusing shadow on Pushkin's poem and Glinka's opera.

Pushkin himself in later years was dissatisfied with his youthful work. Glinka tells us in his memoirs that "at one of Zhukovsky's evenings Pushkin, speaking of his poem 'Ruslan and Lyudmila,' said he would like to make many alterations in it; I wanted to learn from him just what changes he proposed to make, but his untimely end prevented me from doing so." Elsewhere he says, "I had hoped to draw up the scenario under Pushkin's guidance, but was prevented by his untimely end."

Pushkin's tragic death (on January 29-February 10, 1837) was a serious blow to Glinka; as we shall see, he was obliged to fall back on what amounted almost to a committee of librettists, who between them contrived to reduce a tale, already fantastic and inconsequent, to complete incoherence.

"The first thought of 'Ruslan and Lyudmila' was given me by our well-known humourist, Prince Shakhovsky," Glinka tells us. "According to him, the rôle of Chernomor ought to have been written for Vorobieva" [the celebrated contralto, wife of the bass Petrov, who actually took the part of Ratmir with enormous success]. "Ayvazovsky [the marine painter] gave me three Tatar melodies, two of which I used for the *lezginka* and the third for the Andante of Ratmir's scena in Act III of the opera."* Even long before this, he had picked up two other exotic melodies that could now be woven into the score. During a holiday in Finland in 1829 "one of the Finnish postillions sang a song that greatly pleased me; I made him repeat it over and over again and, having fixed it in my memory, used it subsequently as the chief theme of Finn's ballad in 'Ruslan and Lyudmila.' . . . In the autumn of the same year, at Shterich's, I heard a Persian song, sung by a secretary of the Ministry for Foreign Affairs, Khozrev Mirza. This motive served me for the Persian chorus in 'Ruslan.'"

---

* This last was also used by Ferdinand David in "Le Désert" (produced in 1844).

Still earlier, in 1827, he had written an Aria in A flat for baritone, to words by A. Y. Rimsky-Korsakov, "the *adagio* of which I was able to use for the canon in the finale of Act I," one of the finest things in the whole opera.

In December, 1837, eleven months after Pushkin's death, Glinka told his mother that all his thoughts were "centred on the new opera." And he must have begun the music during the next few months, for during the summer he was sent to the Ukraine on official business and while staying with his friend Tarnovsky, who maintained a private orchestra on his estate at Kachenovka, "I found in my portfolio a couple of numbers written (I don't know when) for 'Ruslan': the Persian Chorus and Chernomor's March; I heard both these pieces for the first time at Kachenovka—played very well; in Chernomor's March we substituted wine-glasses for the glockenspiel." During the same visit (June, 1838) "my old school-friend, N. A. Markovich [poet and historian] helped me with [the words of] Finn's ballad, shortening it and imitating [Pushkin's style in] as many verses as were necessary to round off the piece. . . . When the ballad was finished, I sang it time after time with the orchestra."

The next two numbers to be composed were Gorislava's cavatina (by November, 1838) and Lyudmila's cavatina in Act I (by the spring of 1839). And at this stage in the work Glinka at last began to turn his attention to the not unimportant matter of the libretto. Hitherto he had simply been writing music for points in the action that appealed to him, trusting that they could be fitted into the whole later, and adapting or imitating Pushkin's verses to suit his purpose. But an unrhymed narrative poem, not even divided into stanzas, is very far from being a practicable libretto, and so far Glinka had not even sketched out a rough dramatic scenario.

The almost incredible history of the scenario and libretto is extraordinarily confused, owing to the discrepancies between Glinka's memoirs and letters and his friend Kukolnik's diary. (Neither memoirs nor diary is a completely reliable document.) Glinka tells us in his memoirs that he had been introduced to a certain Staff-Captain Shirkov "as a person quite capable of writing a libretto for my new opera. He was indeed a very cultured and talented fellow; he sketched beautifully and wrote verses with great facility. At my request he wrote, by way of trial, Gorislava's cavatina [in Act III] and part of the first act. The trial was very satisfactory, but instead of thinking out the whole plan and action of the piece beforehand, I at once set to work at the cavatinas of Lyudmila and Gorislava, not bothering at all about the dramatic action, but supposing that all this could be settled afterwards." In the postscript of a letter to N. A. Markovich, dated September 20-October 2, 1838, he says, "My poet has finished the first act and begun the second very successfully." Then, some seven weeks after this, occurred a picturesque incident narrated by both Kukolnik and the composer, when the poetaster Bakhturin "undertook to draw up the plan of the opera and, alhough drunk, did so in a quarter of an hour."

But a love-affair, domestic troubles, ill-health and a lifelong tendency to indolence interfered sadly with the progress of the opera. We hear nothing more of it till August, 1840, when Glinka writes to Shirkov: "I have never written so much and never yet felt such inspiration. I implore you, write the fourth act in accordance with the programme sent you; while I am in the country I will go into it with you in still more detail." A fortnight later he does write again from the country (Novospasskoe), begging Shirkov to "set to work first of all with the fifth act, particularly *with the duet* and *with the finale*. According to my reckoning, I've still got two months' work in the writing out of what is already composed; if you can then let me have the fifth act, the thing will go with a swing." And he encloses a "programme" explaining that "except the march and dances" there is as yet no music for Act IV, "so the poet has *carte blanche*," describing what he wants for the finale of that act, and specifying the numbers required for Act V.

Glinka also tells us in his memoirs that, during his stay in the country he wrote the Introduction to

"Ruslan" in three weeks*, and that on the way back to Petersburg in one feverish night he devised the finale of the opera. During the greater part of September and October he temporarily abandoned his opera to write incidental music for Kukolnik's "Prince Kholmsky." In November he was ill. It was not till December that he took up "Ruslan" again, writing the scene of Lyudmila in Chernomor's castle (Act IV), the chorus of flowers, etc., and on February 18-March 2 (1841) he sent Shirkov, with the scenario of Act V, the following account of the state of affairs:—

"*Already written:* (Act I) 1. Introduction, 2. Lyudmila's aria: (Act II). 3. Finn's ballad, 4. Ruslan's aria: (Act III). 5. Persian chorus. 6. Gorislava's cavatina: (Act IV). 7. Fragments from Lyudmila's scene, viz., the chorus of flowers and the *andante* [later marked adagio in the score]. 8. Chernomor's march: (Act V). 9. Ratmir's romance. *In preparation:* (a) Finale of first act. (b) Scene of the head (second act). (c) Dances (third act). (d) Lyudmila's scene and dances (fourth act). (e) Final chorus of the fifth act. *Not begun:* 1. Farlaf's scene with Naina (second act). 2. Ratmir's aria. 3. Finale (third act). 4. Fight and finale (fourth act). 5. Sleep scene. 6. Scene of

---

* The manuscript of Ruslan's big aria in Act III is also dated "September 1, 1840. Novospasskoe."

the killing. 7. Duet. 8. Beginning of the finale (fifth act). . . . The overture and entr'actes can wait till last."*

It would be wearisome and purposeless to follow the further course of the composition during the rest of the year, described in detail in Glinka's letters to Shirkov.† Work was interrupted by the beginning of divorce proceedings against the composer's wife, but the score was completed during the winter and spring, and sent in April, 1842, to A. M. Gedeonov, Director of the Imperial Theatres.

Gedeonov's son, Michael, was a friend of the composer's and the work was dedicated to him. We learn from a letter to Shirkov that "Misha" Gedeonov had altered Glinka's scenario, before the work was completed, in accordance with his father's taste and to make it more practicable scenically.‡ And from a passage in Glinka's memoirs we see that he even became part-librettist: "Shirkov having gone to the Ukraine, Kukolnik and Gedeonov undertook [in September, 1841] to help in the difficult task of making a whole out of the heterogeneous separate parts of my opera. Kukolnik wrote

---

* Glinka tells us in his memoirs that he "wrote the overture directly in full score, much of it in the *Regisseur's* room while rehearsals were going on."

† Glinka's scenarios are very interesting as showing the care he took over the later stages of the libretto.

‡ As it was, drastic cuts had to be made during the rehearsals.

verses* for the finale of the opera and Ratmir's aria in the third act. Gedeonov wrote the little duet between Finn and Ruslan that follows Finn's ballad, Finn's recitative in the third act, and the four-part prayer with which the third act ends. And I myself wrote the scene of Farlaf with Naina and Farlaf's Rondo, as well as the beginning of the finale of the third act. Thus the verses of the libretto, in addition to those taken from Pushkin's poem, were written by Markovich, V. F. Shirkov, Kukolnik, Misha Gedeonov and me."

It is obvious from the foregoing account that the resultant work—performed for the first time on November 27-December 9, 1842, the sixth anniversary of the *première* of "A Life for the Tsar"—is hardly to be judged as a drama. If we can accept it as a still living opera, it is only because the word "opera" is wide enough to cover sins against every canon of Aristotle—and perhaps for the same reason that we do not object to "Kubla Khan" on the ground that it is nonsense. "Ruslan" is a sort of "Kubla Khan" among operas. The magic saves it, and the magic all lies in the music. So let us look a little more closely into the music, this

---

* The following note was written in the margin of the memoirs by Kukolnik: "*In English*. I wrote them in that way so that on Shirkov's return they could be replaced by other verses *with the same meaning*, but this did not happen and now they stand in English." It further appears from Kukolnik's diary that Glinka actually set the English words. I have not been able to discover when and by whom they were afterwards translated into Russian.

music which is the true foundation-stone of the whole Russian school. On almost every page we shall find indications of what was to follow.

Not so much in the slightly Weberian overture, crisp, sparkling little masterpiece though it is, except in the famous descending whole-tone scale near the end. But the opening of the first act, the scene at Svetozar's court, plunges at once into the characeristic atmosphere of "Prince Igor," "Tsar Saltan" and a dozen other Russian masterpieces. It is not only that the song of the bard *(bayan)* and the answering choruses are in "the old Russian heroic style," as Calvocoressi says. (And it must be emphasised that Glinka was the creator rather than the reviver of this broad diatonic style; the *bayan's* song is not very close to the genuine old *bĭlini*, and Rimsky-Korsakov and Borodin owed more to the first scene of "Ruslan" than to the *bĭlini* themselves.) Nor is it of much importance that Glinka's use of piano and harp to suggest the *gusli* later became an accepted convention in "Snegurochka" and other of Korsakov's operas. Or that there are modal touches. The importance of the *bayan's* song is much profounder than this. Some of its phrases seem to contain the germ of all later Russian expression of lyrical emotion, of all the melodious passages where Borodin and Rimsky-Korsakov forget for a moment the accent of folk-song, open their chests, and sing *a piena voce* "from the soul."

Take the phrase to which the *bayan* sings of "the flower of love, of springtime":

Both melodically and harmonically it contains the essence of some of Borodin's most characteristic pages. The slightly facile lyricism of the melody, the simple, delicately tinted harmony, and the transparent, effortless but perfectly effective part-writing seem to have been models for every Russian composer for fifty years after. Or take another passage ("And the token of joy, child of rain and light"):

"Ruslan and Lyudmila."

The chromatic effect of the flattened submediant (sharpened dominant) was the common property of all nineteenth century musicians; but, used as Glinka uses it here, it gave a peculiar *cachet* to Russian harmony. It is not easy to determine *why* the minor triad on the subdominant in the third bar of Ex. 12 has an effect here so different from its effect in, say, Schubert. Yet the difference is hardly deniable. (Perhaps it is because the harmony is only a passing sigh; Schubert would have leaned on it for at least a couple of bars.) And it was certainly from Glinka that later Russian composers learned its voluptuous, half-oriental melancholy.

Lyudmila's cavatina, flawed by pointless bravura passages, though full of character and amusingly pert in the part addressed to Farlaf, is rather disappointing. But the finale of the act is as full of "model" passages as its opening. Comparatively uninspired though it is, the opening of the finale—the half melodic recitatives of Svetozar, Ruslan and Lyudmila in turn, the treatment of the orchestral accompaniment, the melodic outlines and contrapuntal handling of the following ensemble—has served as the pattern for similar passages in nearly every later Russian opera. As for the B major chorus in 5-4 in honour of Lel, the Love God, which follows, it has left the mark of its blazing trills, its rich, curiously hard sonorities:

on any number of Russian compositions in the same key, from the finale of Borodin's Second Symphony to the finale of Stravinsky's "Firebird."

The passing clashes of seconds produced by these inverted pedals seem to have fascinated Glinka and suggested to him the still more daring music of Lyudmila's abduction:

a passage that, on Rimsky-Korsakov's own admission, served as the model for Sadko's descent. Indeed a great deal of Korsakov's "fantastic" music is based on such regular, ruthlessly mathematical patterns as this—its bass descending in whole tones, its upper part in major thirds—and (like the passage leading to the canon of the princes) consists of out-of-the-way chord-progressions pivoting about a single note.

Act II contains some memorable music: Finn's ballad (an even earlier exammple than "Kamarinskaya" of Glinka's favourite "changing background" type of variation, later adopted by Russian composers in general), Ruslan's big aria (part of it familiar as the second subject of the Overture), as Russian and Glinkaesque as Farlaf's *buffo* rondo is Italian and Rossinian, the strikingly conceived scene of the giant head. But as a whole this act has had a less remarkable posterity than the others. Only the scene between Farlaf and the witch Naina seems harmonically (as in Exs. 80 and 81b) and in figuration to anticipate some of Rimsky-Korsakov's dabblings in magic, e.g., in "Christmas Eve" and the "Baba Yaga's hut" theme of his orchestral "Skazka."

But there can be no question of the historical importance of the Persian Chorus that opens Act III. It is one of the loveliest things in the whole score and as interesting as it is beautiful. Though the melody was Persian in origin, it is not strikingly oriental and it has served as the model for a number of non-oriental "maidens' choruses" and dances of the *khorovod* type from those in Korsakov's "May

Night" and "Mlada" to the princesses' dance in "The Firebird." Like Finn's ballad, the Persian chorus is a brilliant example of the " changing background" type of variation. The chorus of girls simply sings the melody over and over again unaltered, *unisono*, but the accompaniment is typical of Glinka's fertility of invention at its best, rich in device and colour (both harmonic and orchestral). The arabesque ornamentation of the variation at the words, " Beauties here will swarm about you " :

is the historic prototype of " Islamey," " Tamara," " Scheherazade " and " The Golden Cockerel," indeed of nearly all Russian essays in pseudo-orientalism.

At the same time it is easy to exaggerate the importance of the orientalism in " Ruslan "—or for that matter in Russian music in general. Despite his use of a certain amount of genuine eastern

"Ruslan and Lyudmila."

material, Glinka's orientalism is little more than a convention, though in justice to him it must be said that he was the inventor of the convention : the triplet arabesques, the luscious, languorous scoring and tonalities. It is worth noting that Ratmir's aria in Act III, the first part of which is a genuine Tatar melody, has left a much smaller mark on later Russian music (except on some of Borodin's themes) than his romance in Act V, " She is life to me, she is joy to me," with its middle section, " Many beauties have loved me " :

which seems to be entirely spurious. The D flat of Ratmir's romance and the D major of the languorous Turkish Dance in 6-8 time in Act IV were obviously the origin of Balakirev's infatuation with those keys and their relative minors.

If the Persian Chorus is rich in the ore that the "mighty handful" afterwards mined so profitably, the rest of the Third Act is hardly less so. The overlapping motives introducing Gorislava's recitative, the chromatic figure introduced in the accompaniment to her romance, the little demisemiquaver ornament in Ratmir's aria, the orchestral accompaniment* to the song of the harem-girls as they surround Ratmir (closely anticipating a passage in "Tsar Saltan")—all these contributed elements to the formation of the characteristic "Russian style." And it is only just to point out that if later composers were indebted to Glinka for so many of their most attractive traits, he must also be debited with some of the weaker ones. Rimsky-Korsakov might have hesitated about the smooth, insipid ensembles of "The Tsar's Bride" and still weaker works if Glinka had not offered him such precedents as the quartet that closes Act III of "Ruslan."

The first noteworthy passage in Act IV is the delicious chorus of flowers—again in the warm, "languorous" key of D flat. This act—particularly this scene and the fight between Ruslan and Chernomor—is the only part of the work (except perhaps the "magic dances" in Act III and the finale of the last act), showing traces of Weber's musical influ-

---

* A folk-tune already used by Glinka in his "Capriccio on Russian Themes" for piano duet (1834).

ence, i.e., of "Oberon" and "Euryanthe." But the Weberian influence is slight enough even here and Weber would never have written such a passage as this one in the fight scene :

What Weber did write may be seen in "Oberon" : the accompaniment to Fatima's "Horch, Herrin, horch!" in the finale of Act I, the passage that obviously suggested Ex. 17 to Glinka.

Certainly there is nothing in the least Weberian about the lullaby just before Chernomor's appearance, a genuine Russian lullaby.* As for Chernomor's march, it is no wonder that Liszt was so struck by it that he hastened to transcribe it for piano. It is absolutely original. Glinka produces a bizarre effect by purely melodic means :

---

* Cf., those in Tchaïkovsky's "Nutcracker" and Stravinsky's "Firebird." Rimsky-Korsakov seems to have unconsciously recollected bars 7 and 8 in the last act of "Snegurochka" (Snegurochka's ecstatic phrase, "O my hero and friend").

though in the trio it is the harmonic aspect that attracts attention:

precursor of some of Korsakov's fantastic ingenuities, notably the Astrologer's music in "The Golden Cockerel."

Of the oriental dances that follow, all of them interesting, the Caucasian *lezginka* is outstanding. Harmonically it is one of the most astonishing products of the first half of the nineteenth century, certainly one of the most daring. The last part, containing such audacities as:

was always cut at the Maryinsky Theatre; it remained too "modern" for official ears three-quarters of a century after it was written. But it has left indelible marks on other Russian masterpieces from "Prince Igor" (dance of the Polovtsian boys) to "The Rite of Spring." Constant Lambert has pointed out that* "the 'Adoration de la Terre' section at the end of the first tableau in 'Le Sacre' is foreshadowed in the offending passage of 'Ruslan,' while the almost equally revolutionary 'Cortège of the Elders' which precedes it can be traced back (through the wizard's procession in 'Firebird' and other pieces) to the march which accompanies the wizard Chernomor in Glinka's opera."

On the whole the Fifth Act is disappointing. Ratmir's romance has already been mentioned; and the little orchestral coda to the Ratmir-Finn duet is worth noting as it obviously served Rimsky-Korsakov as the model for parallel passages in "Snegurochka." The finale, heavily drawn on in the Overture, is brilliant and the introduction in it of a theme from the *lezginka* both ingenious and effective. But it can hardly be said that the opera ends at the highest peak of Glinka's achievement.

In one point, and one only, "Ruslan" is less advanced than "A Life for the Tsar." Glinka had used leitmotives freely and with fine dramatic effect in his earlier opera, but in "Ruslan' they are employed hardly at all. Chernomor's whole-tone scale is really the only leitmotive in the opera. On the other hand, the musical characterisation is far more consistent in the later work. It is not only that

---

* Article in "The Radio Times," May 24, 1935.

Lyudmila's music is generally frivolous, Farlaf's ridiculous, Ratmir's oriental, Svetozar's broad and with a hint of the archaic, dimly foreshadowing Prince Yury's in "Kitezh." All the characters, even minor ones such as Finn, have genuine musical existence and musical personalities. In fact they hardly exist at all outside their music.

III.—GLINKA, DARGOMÏZHSKY AND "THE RUSALKA."

The names of Glinka and Dargomïzhsky are so often bracketed together that it seems worth while to glance briefly at their personal and artistic relationship, and hence at Dargomïzhsky's claim to have made an independent contribution to the foundation of the Russian national school. Glinka was the older man; no one has even suggested that he was influenced in any way by Dargomïzhsky. On the other hand, Dargomïzhsky's most celebrated work, "The Stone Guest," obviously owes nothing to Glinka. But the question still remains: Did the earlier Dargomïzhsky come under Glinka's influence? Was he, as is sometimes asserted, a "follower" of Glinka? Or can it be claimed for him that the small but influential talent he invested in the *kuchkist* stock was entirely his own? Glinka died in 1857 before the "mighty handful" had made its appearance; he had known only one of its members—Balakirev—and him but slightly. Dargomïzhsky was, at any rate during his last year or two, on friendly terms with the whole circle. Personally, then, he was one of their main links with Glinka. Can he be considered in any way a musical link?

In his short autobiography, written in 1866, Dargomïzhsky gives the following account of his personal relations with the older composer: "I made Glinka's acquaintance in 1833. We saw each other three or four times a week, and after a couple of months we called each other 'thou.' . . . We played piano duets a great deal together and analysed the scores of Beethoven's symphonies and Mendelssohn's overtures. A common culture, a common love of art immediately drew us together, and we soon formed a sincere friendship, notwithstanding that Glinka was ten years older than I." (Glinka was then thirty, Dargomïzhsky twenty.) "For twenty-two years our relations were always most close and most friendly. Our friendship was not shaken even during the last years of Mikhail Ivanovich's life when, as so often happens, acquaintances came along who tried their best to arouse mutual artistic jealousy between us. Glinka's culture and my sincere respect for his talent triumphed over tittle-tattle. 'A Life for the Tsar' was already half written. I was enraptured by it. . . . Glinka's example and the sensible advice of N. V. Kukolnik led me to study the theory of music. Glinka gave me Professor Dehn's theoretical manuscripts which he had brought with him from Berlin [five note-books containing, in German, a course of counterpoint and instrumentation in Glinka's own handwriting]. I copied them out with my own hand, quickly mastered the so-called supreme wisdom of thorough-bass and counterpoint . . . . and busied myself with the study of orchestration. My first essays in orchestration were made for concerts that Glinka and I arranged for charity. The essays were successful."

And in a letter of September, 1848, to Prince Kastrioto-Skanderbek, after enquiring what Glinka is doing, Dargomïzhsky says: "I consider his productions very important, not only for Russian music but for music in general. Everything that comes from his pen is new and interesting." Elsewhere he expresses even greater enthusiasm, particularly for "Ruslan." The dilettante composer, V. T. Sokolov, tells us that "at Dargomïzhsky's evenings many of Glinka's songs were sung, as well as numbers from 'A Life for the Tsar' and 'Ruslan,' and, in addition to the overtures and dances from both operas, both the Spanish overtures, the 'Valse-fantaisie,' the overture and entr'actes from 'Prince Kholmsky,' etc., were played in piano duet form. The public at that time did not value or understand 'Ruslan.' Alexander Sergeevich [Dargomïzhsky] always said that 'Ruslan' was incomparably higher than 'A Life for the Tsar.' Does this sound like a desire to depreciate Glinka?"

But, all the same, it seems rather doubtful whether their relations were quite as cordial as Dargomïzhsky says. In the whole of Glinka's correspondence very few letters to Dargomïzhsky have been preserved; indeed when Findeisen published the "Collected Letters" in 1908, he could find only one, though a few more have come to light since. In the whole of Glinka's memoirs there is only one reference to the younger man (on the occasion of their first meeting, when he speaks of him as "a fine pianist and later a very talented composer"). And Lyudmila Shestakova (*née* Glinka), in her account of her brother's last years, gives a less idyllic account of their personal and artistic relations*: "A. S. Dargomïzhsky came to see my brother fairly often [she is speaking of the winter 1854-55], and usually my brother was very glad to see him, but their intercourse was not without various sallies on my brother's part. At that time Dargomïzhsky was writing his 'Rusalka' and used to bring my brother what he had written for him to hear. My brother admired a great deal in this opera, but when Dargomïzhsky sang him the Princess's aria in the third act, my brother said: 'That's very like Gorislava's

---

* That they often got on badly has been confirmed by P. A. Stepanov and others who knew them both. But the evidence concerning their personal relations is on some points flatly contradictory.

aria in the third act of 'Ruslan.'"* Dargomïzhsky did not wish to quarrel with my brother and very pleasantly passed it off in a joke: 'Well, brother, all sorts of strangers pilfer from you, so why shouldn't one of your own friends help himself now and again?' On another occasion, when Dargomïzhsky was not in a very good humour, he replied angrily to my brother's remark that one of the motives from 'The Rusalka' recalled another composer: 'You imagine it, or else you're simply making it up.' My brother persuaded Dargomïzhsky to begin a comic opera as soon as he had finished this one, saying he was sure it would turn out a *chef d'œuvre*. But strangely enough Dargomïzhsky always seemed affronted by this and once even said to him: 'You really think I can't do anything but comic things?' My brother told him that, of course, he could see very well that there were also excellent non-comic things in 'The Rusalka,' but that in his opinion it was by no means easier to write a comic opera, indeed that it called for a special talent which he found in him alone."

Nevertheless Dargomïzhsky took Glinka's advice and began what he called a "Russian magical-comic opera, "Rogdana," though he never finished it, the dropping of "The Rusalka" from the repertoire having made him lose hope of the production of a new opera from his pen. When he returned to

---

* Glinka's criticism was hardly justified; the two songs are alike in nothing but general mood.

opera, it was with a work of an entirely new kind: the famous "Stone Guest." But the often quoted letter to Prince Odoevsky—written in July, 1855, when "The Rusalka" was finished (all but the overture) and the composer was scoring it—is in rather curious contrast with his protest to Glinka: "The more I study the elements of our folk-music, the more varied are the sides I find to it. Glinka, who alone so far has given Russian music broad dimensions, has in my opinion as yet touched only one side of it—the lyrical side. With him the drama is too lugubrious; the comic side loses its national character." (There is some truth in that: cf. Farlaf's aria in "Ruslan.") "I am speaking only of the character of his music, for the *facture* is always superb. As far as I am able, I am working in my 'Rusalka' at the development of our dramatic elements. I shall be happy if I succeed in this only half as well as Glinka."

"The Rusalka" certainly owes something to "A Life for the Tsar" in general characteristics, but little in detail, next to nothing in inspiration, and comparatively little in technical handling. Findeisen is right in saying that the style of the opera is far nearer to "A Life for the Tsar" than to "La Juive" and "Robert le Diable," which had influenced Dargomïzhsky's earlier works, "Esmeralda" (finished 1839; produced 1847), and "The Triumph of Bacchus" (begun 1840; produced 1867). But that was only natural. Yet where Dargomïzhsky does follow Glinka he produces only a feeble imitation of him, colourless where Glinka is colourful, clumsy where Glinka is light-handed, diffuse and pointless where Glinka is concise. Dargomïzhsky arouses interest only where he steps on ground that Glinka had not ventured to tread (e.g., the psychological subtlety of the musical portrait of the Miller), or where he develops a mere hint of Glinka's (e.g., in "The Stone Guest," where instead of contenting himself with the whole-tone scale *à la* "*Ruslan*," he launches out for a few bars into the whole-tone mode, harmonies and all).

Yet we must not under-estimate the importance of "The Rusalka" in the history of Russian music, an oasis of a sort in the twenty years' desert between Glinka's last big work ("Ruslan": produced in 1842) and the earliest important compositions of the "mighty handful." It was, as Findeisen says, "the first serious Russian opera after Glinka"[*] and it produced a powerful impression on sensitive contemporaries. V. T. Sokolov, at that time a complete Italianophile, was completely bewildered by the first performance and left the theatre "with his head in a state of chaos"; he returned again and again to this revolutionary work and realised the composer's "genius" only after five or six hearings. We hear of Glinka himself weeping over a duet (presumably

---

[*] It was begun in the summer of 1848, abandoned on account of difficulties with the libretto, resumed in June, 1852, completed in the summer of 1855, and performed for the first time on May 4-16, 1856, shortly after Glinka had left Russia for the last time.

that in Act I) in "The Rusalka"—which suggests that Glinka's tears flowed rather easily. And we know that even in our day the part of the Miller could be made effective by a genius who happened to be a great actor as well as a great singer.

Yet, turning the pages of the score in cold blood, it is difficult to find anything of more than the mildest interest. One notes the accurate, unconventional declamation of the recitatives; Dargomïzhsky's vaunted "dramatic truth" is much more conspicuous than his equally vaunted humour. (Even the marriage-broker's music seems rather feeble.) One pauses over the Weberian introduction to the Rusalka's scena in the last act:

which, with part of the chorus of rusalkas, on Rimsky-Korsakav's own confession, exercised some influence on the section of his early "musical picture,"

"Sadko," describing the Sea King's feast. But on the whole one gets the impression of a work differing very little in anything but technical accomplishment from the numerous dilettante Russian operas that preceded "A Life for the Tsar" and very definitely inferior to that work in musical quality. As for "Ruslan," "The Rusalka" is not to be compared with it. Dargomïzhsky's work belongs to a past age and, except for the recitatives and the solitary case just mentioned, appears not to have exercised the slightest influence on the music of the next generation. As an influence, Dargomïzhsky came to life first with his orchestral fantasias (and to a certain extent with his songs) and then with "The Stone Guest."

IV.—DARGOMÏZHSKY'S ORCHESTRAL PIECES.

"*Dargomïzhsky?*" reflected Tchaïkovsky in his diary (July 23, 1888). "Yes! He certainly had talent! But he is the supreme example of the dilettante in music. . . . D. was completely wanting in mastery (he hadn't a tenth part of Glinka's). But he had a certain piquancy and originality. He was particularly successful in harmonic *curiosities*." The judgment is not altogether unjust, but, coming from a composer who was under a certain debt to Dargomïzhsky, it is distinctly ungenerous. The finale of Tchaïkovsky's Second Symphony, the "Danse baroque" of his Second Orchestral Suite (actually marked "in Dargomïzhsky's style"), the "Russian Dance" in "Nutcracker," all owe a great deal to Dargomïzhsky's "Kazachok." And not only Tchaïkovsky, but Mussorgsky, Rimsky-Korsakov and Cui were equally influenced by this "typical dilettante."

Dargomïzhsky was Mussorgsky's forerunner in the introduction of satire and realism in the art-song. Mussorgsky's "Marriage" (and, to a less extent, "Boris") and Korsakov's "Maid of Pskov" and "Mozart and Salieri" were strongly influenced by Dargomïzhsky's last opera, the famous (but quite unknown) "Stone Guest." And the dry pungent harmony characteristic of so much Russian "fantastic" music (from Mussorgsky's "Night on the Bare Mountain" to "The Golden Cockerel" and "The Firebird") owning Glinka's "Ruslan" as one parent, must admit Dargomïzhsky as the other. Those "harmonic curiosities"—and not only the whole-tone music in "The Stone Guest"—opened the way, through Mussorgsky, Korsakov and Stravinsky, to things that are now the common property of all modern musicians.

Of all Dargomïzhsky's works, the only ones the English listener has a chance to hear are his three orchestral pieces, the "Kazachok," "Baba Yaga," and the "Fantasia on Finnish Themes." True, his earlier opera, "The Rusalka" (1856) has been done over here (largely because it had a fine rôle for Chaliapin), but "The Stone Guest" is regarded as a museum-piece even in Russia, and Dargomïzhsky's most characteristic songs depend too much on their "truthful" interpretation of the Russian words to be very effective in translation. But the three orchestral pieces seem to be belatedly gaining a foot-hold on the brink of the repertoire, at any rate of the broadcast repertoire.

These three works all date from the same period, the early eighteen-sixties, when the idea of "The Stone Guest" had already occurred to Dargomïzhsky, but five or six years before he began its composition. After "The Rusalka" he had begun a "Russian magical-comic" opera, "Rogdana," but on February 4-11, 1863,* he wrote to Glinka's old friend, N. V. Kukolnik: "I've finally abandoned the comic opera I had begun. I am writing a number of characteristic fantasias for orchestra. For example, a polonaise, a *kazachok* [Cossack dance], a Russian legend, a Finnish dance, etc. The novelty of these elements may find favour abroad, where I have long turned in my dreams." Two years later the dreams partly came true. On January 7 (N.S.), 1865, Dargomïzhsky had the joy of hearing his "Kazachok," with the rather Weberian "Rusalka" Overture, played in the Salle Grande Harmonie, Brussels. (It had an excellent reception from both public and press.) But "Baba Yaga" and the Finnish Fantasia were never played in his lifetime, even in Russia.†

Of the three pieces the "Little-Russian Kaza-

---

* Rimsky-Korsakov says in the chapter of his memoirs devoted to "1861-62," that at this period the Balakirev circle "considered Dargomïzhsky's three orchestral fantasias as mere curiosities." The three "curiosities" did not exist at that period and even the "Kazachok" was not performed in Russia till November, 1865 (in Moscow).

† Balakirev conducted the first performance of the Finnish piece at a Petersburg concert of the Russian Music Society on February 22/March 6, 1869, a month or so after the composer's death. The programme opened with the first Russian performance of Schubert's "Unfinished" Symphony and ended with the first Russian performance of the "Meistersinger" overture.

chok" is by far the most successful. Its indebtedness to Glinka's "Kamarinskaya" is obvious. (Both pieces consist almost entirely of incessant variations on rather trivial little dance tunes.) Dargomïzhsky never treated the instruments as Glinka did, "with understanding of their most secret resources" (as Berlioz said); his orchestration, though generally effective and often novel, lacks polish and subtlety. Whereas Glinka's scoring is always bright and pellucid, Dargomïzhsky's is often thick and sometimes badly miscalculated. The same clumsy but uncontional amateurishness shows itself in his harmonic texture. Glinka, amateur though he was, was at least a master of clear, simple, effective part-writing, but Dargomïzhsky generally writes most awkwardly when he attempts a straightforward piece of harmonisation (e.g., the slow passage near the opening of the "Kazachok"). On the other hand, he excels in the orchestral presentation of a bare harmonic sketch, as in this passage near the end of the "Kazachok":

where the piquancy of the "harmonic curiosity" distracts attention from everything else.

Dargomïzhsky revels in the dry, astringent quality of such effects of augmented or diminished fifths or fourths; they are the foundation of most of his "harmonic curiosities." Indeed, when he leaves them alone, his harmony all too often lapses into unadventurous manipulation of common chords. Chopin and Liszt and the chromatic harmonic world they called into existence meant nothing to Dargomïzhsky. Though the most daring of adventurers, his starting-point was not Chopin but Haydn or Clementi. At the same time, the little harmonic territory that he conquered is unmistakably his own. The harmonic flavour gives Dargomïzhsky's own music individuality, and when one meets it in Mussorgsky or Rimsky-Korsakov, one feels at once (if one knows his music), "Ah, that comes from Dargomïzhsky."

Dargomïzhsky's music is also marked, more strongly than anyone's except Mussorgsky's, with grotesque humour. The "Kazachok" is full of boisterous Gogolian humour, a comic sense expressing itself in unexpected syncopations, in instrumental effects (e.g., quick passage work for two bassoons only), and even in harmonic surprises:

23 fag., tromb., etc.

"Baba Yaga" is humorous, too; the composer called it frankly a "comic fantasia." The witch Baba Yaga was a fearsome creature. According to W. R. S. Ralston ("The Songs of the Russian People": London, 1872), "she is generally represented under the form of a hideous old woman, very tall in stature, very long of limb, with an excessively long nose, and with dishevelled hair.... Her usual habitation is a cottage which stands 'on fowls' legs,' that is, on slender supports.... When the Baba Yaga goes abroad, she rides in an iron mortar. This she propels with the pestle ... and as she goes she sweeps away the traces of her passage with a broom." But like most of the other evil characters of Russian folk-lore, including the Devil himself, she is generally a semi-comic creature, though none of the composers who have followed Dargomïzhsky in depicting her—Mussorgsky, Rimsky-Korsakov and Lyadov—has treated her quite as disrespectfully as he has done.

His fantasia bears the sub-title "from the Volga to Riga." Beginning with a series of variations on the well-known folk-song, "Down by Mother Volga," it then depicts the witch's flight across Russia to the least Russian part of the Tsar's empire: the German-speaking Baltic provinces, "the land," as Findeisen says, "of domesticity, gossip and beer." The orchestra announces her arrival by playing a German folk-song, "Anna Maria, so gehst du doch hin." But the sedate tune is quickly caught up in the most fantastic variations; one gets the impression that Baba Yaga is performing a wild, malicious dance over the sleeping roofs of Riga; and the piece ends with the violin shrieks *(près de la poigner)* that have punctuated her flight through the air.

The most interesting part of this rather naïve essay in programme-music is the middle section depicting the ride, which shares with Liszt's "Totentanz" the parentage of nearly all Russian witches' sabbaths and the like, from Mussorgsky's "Night on the Bare Mountain" onwards. Accompanied almost throughout by repeated notes on the bass drum *ppp*, the whole episode sounds astonishingly modern, for Dargomïzhsky made the most of the opportunity for harmonic ruthlessness. It is almost incredible that such a passage as this:

was written in 1863.

The "Finnish Fantasia" is a more important work. Indeed Borodin considered it "decidedly the best of Dargomïzhsky's orchestral pieces"; his impression is worth quoting, both for its indication of the attitude of the younger Russians to Dargomïzhsky and for its expression of a typical Russian view of the Finnish national character. Describing the memorable R.M.S. concert referred to above—he was acting critic of the "St. Petersburg Vedomosti" (*vice* Cui)—Borodin said: "The Fantasia is based on Finnish folk-tunes and depicts Finns in holiday mood who first sing one of their melancholy songs (Introduction, F sharp minor, 5-4), then, becoming more cheerful, begin to dance*—at first quietly but little by little warming up to the extreme limits of Finnish boldness and Finnish passion—empty, feeble, clumsy and comic in the highest degree (Allegretto, A major, 2-4). It is impossible to give in words any idea of all the humour of this delightful musical picture. Dargomïzhsky here shows himself as great a genre-painter as in his humorous songs ('The Worm,' 'The Titular Councillor,' and others). As regards the technical beauties of the music, the 'Finnish Fantasia' offers rich material for study in spite of its small scale. It is crammed full of completely original passages and effects—harmonic, instrumental and rhythmic. One finds musical curiosities of the most unprecedented, most diverse kinds, at every step; it is utterly impossible to enumerate them in detail—one

---

* Findeisen says Dargomïzhsky composed the piece "at his summer villa in the village of Murino, near Petersburg, where he had probably seen Finns dancing clumsily in this way."

would be obliged to pause at almost every bar of the piece. And the whole thing sparkles with inimitable humour and wit. The 'Finnish Fantasia' is decidedly the best of Dargomïzhsky's orchestral pieces. The impression it made on the public was clearly expressed by the unanimous applause and cries of 'encore,' after which the piece was repeated."

Borodin hardly exaggerates the "curious" element in the score, though the "wit" is less apparent and the humour seems rather thin. (Our view of Sibelius's countrymen is not that of a Russian of the 'sixties.) But even its formal structure is interesting. As a genuine musical architect, Dargomïzhsky was little better than childish, but his Fantasia is given a certain coherence by a sort of "dissolving view" effect in the transition from the *andante* to the *allegretto*—the *allegretto* theme being introduced quite early in the *andante*—and by the (quite logical) reappearance of the 5-4 theme twice in the *allegretto*, thundered out by the trombones. Incidentally this last passage provides a typical instance of Dargomïzhsky's harmonic experimentation almost implying polytonality:

This 5-4 theme, first stated by the oboe, has a special interest for the student of Russian music. As Constant Lambert was, I think, the first to point out, it "sounds like a dignified version of the drunken monk's song in 'Boris'" (Varlaam's song about the taking of Kazan). The first bar:

is practically identical with the opening of Mussorgsky's melody, and it is perhaps not without significance that the inn-scene of "Boris," in which Varlaam's song occurs, was written early in 1869, at the very time of that memorable R.M.S. concert when the Fantasia was given its first performance.

V.—THE WHOLE-TONE SCALE IN RUSSIAN MUSIC.

There is, on the face of it, no reason why it should not be as natural for a musician to conceive a theme in the whole-tone scale as in a scale in which the intervals between the third and fourth, and seventh and eighth, degrees (or between any other degrees) are semitones. Yet many people are conscious of a feeling—apart altogether from the prejudices of natural conservatism—that music in the whole-tone mode is "made," not born. Nor is the antipathy entirely due to the absence of a key-centre, for it is much easier (for some of us, at any rate) to accept the most advanced chromatic music, which has the same disadvantage. And in either case it is possible to create an artificial tonic, by dwelling on, and returning to, any particular note. Again, there is no a priori reason for considering the whole-tone scale more artificial than our ordinary major and minor scales or the pentatonic scale or any exotic Persian or Fiji or Hottentot scale under the sun. Yet there is no getting away from the fact that music conceived in the whole-tone mode—Debussy's

The Whole-tone Scale in Russian Music. 63

"Cloches à travers les feuilles," and "Voiles," for instance—does sound artificial. We may even have wondered why the opening theme of "Scheherazade":

sounded "made," and discovered the reason only when we found it was simply a descending whole-tone scale with diatonic trimmings.

Yet we can accept the same scale in Glinka's "Ruslan" Overture* and Borodin's B minor Symphony:

---

* See Ex. 7 in my "Studies in Russian Music."

without turning a hair. It sounds so natural, particularly under these harmonic disguises (until we stop to think about it), that we hardly notice it. And even when we do, it does not slightly offend our musical sense as the Debussy and Rimsky-Korsakov examples do. (We accept the Rimsky-Korsakov because it makes a striking opening and sounds "barbaric" as we say rather vaguely, and whatever pleasure we get from "Cloches à travers les feuilles" is akin to that we feel in listening to clever variations on a vapid theme, the pleasure of hearing a clever man make something out of next to nothing.) In other words, the whole-tone scale sounds unpleasantly artificial only when the actual thematic material is based on it. We don't mind the composer's using it in the process of "composition," but we find it difficult to believe that it had any natural connection with his "inspiration."

I think it can be shown that this is not due to mere prejudice. Just as an idea occurs to an Englishman in terms of English words, natural musical ideas occur to a composer in the musical idiom generally current at the time in his part of the world. Musical innovations appear first in what we can only call the composer's "resources," where his processes are intellectual rather than instinctive—above all in his harmony. Not until they are naturalised there do they begin to affect the real essence of music. Only Tristanesque harmony made possible Schönberg's

The Whole-tone Scale in Russian Music. 65

melody; that is, made it *naturally* possible. We feel that it is unnatural for a composer to be "inspired" in the whole-tone scale because the whole-tone scale is not yet a part of the current idiom. Lest this should sound too much like the case of the boy who was not allowed to go into the water until he had learned to swim, we must return to the language parallel. Though an idea occurs to an Englishman in English words, in order to express it fully or precisely or vividly he may have to use foreign words or phrases, or he may even be compelled, as scientists often are, to *invent* terms. In the course of time the foreign terms become naturalised or the invented ones are generally accepted and incorporated in the language, and after that it is perfectly natural for a spontaneous idea to come clothed in them.

Obviously, a great deal can be learned from a study of the works of the first composers to experiment with a device, and the use of the whole-tone scale by the classical Russian masters well repays examination, for their practice defines its possibilities and limitations fairly clearly. Almost invariably they treat it simply as an auxiliary means of expression, not as a self-contained language, but as one uses foreign words to augment one's vocabulary. They are content to weave a single strand of whole-tone music through a diatonic web, to build diatonic chord-progressions on a whole-tone foundation, as in the Glinka and Borodin examples quoted,* or, as Rimsky-Korsakov has done in the opening of "Scheherazade," to use the scale as the skeleton of a diatonic melody. And, curiously enough, it is nearly always the scale itself which they use—in nine cases out of ten the descending scale—not a melodic line derived from it.

A typical example may be found in Borodin's song, "The Sleeping Princess," where the scale, first in crotchets as a bass, then in minims as a middle part, underlines the references to "the wood spirits who pass with cries and laughter, without breaking the spell," and to the fearless prince who *will* come one day and break it. In the same composer's "Falshivaya Nota" ("The False Note") a rising bass figure in whole-tones similarly emphasises the vital lines: "She swore that she loved me—I did not believe her. *A false note sounded in her voice and in her heart.* And she knew this herself." But here again its function is simply to underline, not to express the emotional discord of which the singer is conscious.

An even more instructive example from Borodin is the *lento* theme for trombones which interrupts the Finale of his B minor Symphony (see Ex. 29). When it is repeated two bars later (a tone lower) a semitone already slips in (G natural instead of G

---

* Though Glinka uses the augmented triad, the "common chord" of the whole-tone scale, with it in the fourth act of "Ruslan."

The Whole-tone Scale in Russian Music. 67

flat), though this may be a mistake in the score. But when the strings take it up in the quick *tempo* it is frankly diatonic:

It is, in fact, only this transformation (with the pedal D of the horns) which enables us to say definitely that Ex. 29 is a genuine whole-tone conception, since its range is confined to four notes and is therefore possible within the limits of the ordinary major scale. The interesting point is that the composer throws the whole-tone scale overboard directly he wants to develop his theme, just as Rimsky-Korsakov does in the first movement of "Scheherazade." Indeed, Ex. 30 sounds so natural and spontaneous that it is safe to assume that it was Borodin's original conception, and Ex. 29 the derivative form. With the exception of some unimportant examples in the finale of "Mlada," one of his least interesting compositions, there is no instance in Borodin's music of actual thematic material conceived or devised in the whole-tone mode.

Even as a means of expression, the Russians seem to have found that the whole-tone scale had a very limited usefulness. At the risk of being accused of adding to the arbitrary code which associates the minor mode with sadness, chromatic scales with storms and tempests, and grunts on the bass tuba with dragons, one cannot help pointing out that in Russian music the scale is almost always used to express or symbolise the hard, harsh, or rigorous. In "Ruslan and Lyudmila,'" for instance, Glinka associates it with Chernomor. Dargomïzhsky found an admirable pretext for using it fairly extensively in his "Stone Guest"* as the symbol of the stone statue of the Commander. But Dargomïzhsky was, first and foremost, an intellectual composer, and although Balakirev's circle professed to take his "Stone Guest" as their "gospel," they treated it in practice more as a standard of reference than as a model. Rimsky-Korsakov introduces a descending whole-tone scale on the brass in the second act of his "May Night" at a point where the headman of the village threatens to put a

---

* For a full account of the use of whole-tone music in "The Stone Guest," see my "Studies in Russian Music," Chapter IV.

The Whole-tone Scale in Russian Music. 69

miscreant in jail and "punish him unmercifully." And the opening of "Scheherazade," according to the composer himself, "depicts Scheherazade's stern spouse."

Again, in the Borodin Symphony, there can hardly be any mistaking the fact that the composer is using the whole-tone mode to express brutal, elemental power. The association of the whole-tone scale with the idea of severity is, in fact, neither more nor less arbitrary than any of the other common associations referred to. But, for good or ill, the association is definitely established in the practice of the classical Russian masters.

Seeing that Rimsky-Korsakov used the whole-tone scale himself it would be interesting to know why he took it upon himself to alter Mussorgsky's F sharps in "Boris Godunov":

31

to F naturals. Scott Goddard, commenting on this in a discussion of the various editions of "Boris"* says: "The tyranny of the text-book is here felt at its strongest. The suppression of one sharp has done more to call into question Rimsky-

---

* "Music and Letters," July, 1929.

Korsakov's right to the title of artist than all his own works have done to support that right. His reason for doing it is too apparent to need any comment. The ancients called the augmented fourth the devil. We may leave it thus." But that cannot be the explanation, for the sharpened fourth is sometimes found in Russian folk-songs, and apart from other instances in "Boris," there are examples in Rimsky-Korsakov's own works. As for *diabolus in musica*, though it is true Korsakov associates the tritone with the devil in his "Christmas Eve," there is plenty of evidence that he was rather fond of its pungent flavour. Another scale met with in Russian folk-music is a form of the major with a flattened seventh. These sharpened fourths and flattened sevenths point directly to the whole-tone scale, and though it is highly improbable that the Russians derived it from these folk-modes, the latter must have made it much easier for their ears to accept it.

That these composers saw few possibilities in the whole-tone mode, even as an additional means of expression, is evident from the infrequency with which they employed it. And it is significant that Stravinsky, who in his earlier works equipped himself with every effective weapon in the Kuchkist armoury, left the whole-tone scale severely alone. The following episode in the "Danse infernale" of "The Firebird" is exceptional :

The Whole-tone Scale in Russian Music. 71

To adduce Skryabin's whole-tone-writing in "The Poem of Ecstasy" and "Prometheus" is not very illuminating, for the whole-tone sequence was to Skryabin not a scale at all, but an arpeggio. Toying with chords derived from the upper partials of the harmonic series, Skryabin lighted fortuitously on whole-tone chords, but, as far as one can see, he never attempted to write "whole-tone music." When, for a few moments, he seems to be doing so, it is simply that he has arpeggioed a chord. He thus stands apart from the classical Russians in this respect as in so many others, for they evidently adopted the scale quite empirically and always regarded it horizontally, to the almost total neglect of its vertical implications.

VI.—ORIENTAL ELEMENTS IN RUSSIAN MUSIC.

The late Cuthbert Hadden, in one of his gossipy books on music and musicians, speaks of the "reliance" of certain Russian composers "on Oriental jingle and clatter." He mentions no names, but it is clear from the context that he is thinking of Rimsky-Korsakov and his allies. That is admittedly a "popular" view, but I fancy it is shared in a modified form by a great many well-informed musicians. They would recognise something more than mere "jingle and clatter" in the orientalism of the Russian classics, and they would want to substitute some other word for "reliance"; but on the whole, I imagine, they would agree as to the importance of the oriental element in the music of Rimsky-Korsakov and Balakirev, to say nothing of Glinka's, Borodin's and Mussorgsky's. Yet, in spite of the evident predilection of Russian composers for quasi-oriental effects, a little examination soon shows that the importance of this element in their music has been greatly exaggerated. The popular view of Rimsky-Korsakov and Balakirev as two-thirds Slav, one-third Oriental in musical mentality is a grotesquely distorted one, due to nothing more than the excessive popularity of the very small proportion of quasi-oriental works in their output. We must remember, too, that "oriental" is a vague term including elements as widely different as Tatar, Caucasian, Armenian, Persian, Kurdish and Arabian (to say nothing of Indian and Far Eastern types which have attracted the Russians hardly at all). Now all these diverse types of music have hardly more in common than the folk-music of England, South Germany and Italy. To lump them together and label them "oriental" is in itself to give a false collective importance to comparatively insignificant separate influences. On the other hand, it must be admitted that the composers themselves have not always been pedantically precise on this point. Balakirev was careful to use only Caucasian and Armenian themes in "Islamey," and Rimsky-Korsakov restricted his borrowings to genuine Arabian melodies in "Antar." But the latter did not hesitate to introduce Persian and Caucasian melodies in the Cleopatra scene of "Mlada."

Still it is undeniable that the oriental element, small as it really is, bulks much larger in Russian music than in that of any other European nation and that the orientalism of Russian composers, if far from accurate scientifically, seems a great deal less superficial than that of such composers as Weber, Bizet and Puccini. And this does appear to demonstrate real sympathy, even affinity, something deeper than mere love of musical fancy-dress. But these facts can be accounted for in another way. Various factors, chiefly the gradual penetration of Central Asia by Russian arms during the last century, had scattered different oriental types all over Russia, even in the far north-west. We know from the composers themselves that they picked up their oriental themes in the most unexpected places. Sometimes, it is true, they deliberately went to "sources." Borodin and Balakirev visited the Caucasus, and Rimsky-Korsakov got the themes of his "Antar" from a French collection of Arabian melodies in Borodin's possession (actually, Salvador-Daniel's) and from Christianovich's collection. But for the most part the authentic oriental melodies in their music are simply tunes which they heard by chance and which caught their fancy. Thus Rimsky-Korsakov heard the Persian melody already mentioned in the northern summer resort of Ligovo; and Balakirev picked up the Armenian melody in "Islamey" (the slower theme in D major) in Moscow, and the quasi-oriental theme in the finale of his First Symphony in a third-class compartment on the Finland Railway.* Again, Rimsky-Korsakov tells us in his memoirs that for the

---

* See page 188.

Oriental Elements in Russian Music. 75

first Allegro of "Tamara" Balakirev "used a melody which we heard together on the occasion of a visit to the barracks of the Imperial Escort. Even now I can see these oriental figures as they strummed this melody on their balalaika- or guitar-like instruments, as well as a variant of the one on which Glinka based his 'Persian Chorus.'"

These details are not as trivial as they appear, for they show how oriental music of one kind or another, as a definitely foreign type of art, was continually being brought before the notice of Russian musicians whether they were specially interested in it or not. It naturally attracted their attention. But—except perhaps in the cases of Borodin and Balakirev, to which we must return in a moment—it is absurd to see anything more than a transient interest and liking in their attitude to it. On the contrary, it is evident that their interest was due not to sympathy or subtle affinity but to the very exoticism of the music. It appealed to them, not because it touched a responsive note in themselves, but because it was so un-Russian. Their use of oriental interludes in their operas, as pure *divertissements* or to produce striking contrasts, shows this very clearly. The oriental scenes in "Ruslan" and the "Persian Dances" in Mussorgsky's "Khovanshchina" are thoroughly typical in this respect. Similarly the trio "alla turca" (on a Kurdish theme) by which Mussorgsky converted his "March of the Princes," from the projected

"Mlada" of 1872, into a symphonic tableau, "The Taking of Kars,"* is as definitely an anti-Russian symbol as the "Marseillaise" in Tchaïkovsky's "1812" and is introduced for precisely the same purpose. But Mussorgsky's interest in the music of the East was very slight. In the whole of his work there are only one or two other unimportant essays in this field.

In all these cases, even where authentic eastern melodies are used, the treatment is purely Russian. One does not expect serious attempts to approximate to the texture of genuine eastern music; composers are not scientific students of musical ethnology. But one cannot speak even of specifically pseudo-oriental harmonic formulas in Russian music. Rimsky-Korsakov, for instance, uses precisely the same harmonic devices to bring out the flavour of oriental melodies and indigenous Russian folk-songs alike. So that even the authentic eastern element in the music is highly stylised and reduced to a convention, less obviously conventional than the pseudo-orientalism of Western composers only because the non-oriental ingredients are so much less familiar and threadbare.

The most successful practitioners of this particular oriental convention (originated by Glinka) were undoubtedly Balakirev and Rimsky-Korsakov. Balakirev's entire musical personality is marked by traits akin to certain characteristics of

---
* See note on page 102.

oriental decorative art—a love of arabesque lines, profusion of minute (but always living) detail, sensuous warmth and exuberance of imagination. Yet only two of his major works are avowedly oriental in nature, and the fact that these two, "Islamey" and "Tamara," are by far the best known of his compositions, the only ones known to a great many people, has given a very false impression of the extent of his preoccupation with eastern subjects. Similarly, people who know nothing of "Sadko" but the all-too-popular "Hindu Song" (another case of purely incidental *divertissement*, and the only quasi-oriental fragment in the whole work) probably have a vague idea that "Sadko" is an opera on an oriental subject. Indeed, thanks largely to the popularity of this song and of "Scheherazade," Rimsky-Korsakov has been even more completely misjudged than Balakirev. The very early ""Fantasia on Serbian Themes" (which scarcely anyone knows, and which is hardly worth knowing),* "Antar," "Scheherazade," the "Indian Dance" and Cleopatra scene in "Mlada," and the music associated with the Queen of Shemakhan and

---

* I mention it here because the themes are definitely non-European in type. Tchaïkovsky commented on this in a newspaper article when the "Fantasia" was first performed. "If the motives are really of Serbian origin" (they are) "it would be interesting to know why these melodies show clear signs of the influence of the music of eastern peoples." Apparently the Slavonic purity of Serbian folk-music had been corrupted by long contact with Turkish culture.

her attendants in "The Golden Cockerel," with a few songs, represent the whole of Rimsky-Korsakov's eastern excursions—very little for such a prolific composer. And even this small bulk is diminished in importance when we examine it and find to what extent he echoes both Balakirev and his own earlier works. The composer himself confessed to reflections of Glinka and Balakirev in "Antar"; the solo violin theme of "Scheherazade" closely resembles a theme in "Tamara"; and the seductions of the Queen of Shemakhan are musically closely modelled on those of Cleopatra. All in all, the oriental elements in Rimsky-Korsakov amount to no more than a few borrowed melodies, a few arabesque melodic formulas, and (possibly) his penchant for rhythmical underlinings with percussion instruments. The fondness for unusual scales and intervals noticeable in so much of his music, popularly supposed to be of eastern origin, is really nothing of the kind. Rimsky-Korsakov's lifelong addiction to a purely artificial kind of "fantastic" music began with his invention for the early symphonic poem, "Sadko," of a scale of alternate whole-tones and semitones. So the appearance of the same scale a little later at the end of the third movement of "Antar" is merely sham orientalism. Rimsky-Korsakov made this "fantastic" idiom of his invention serve many purposes—the representation of the supernatural as contrasted with the human elements in "Sadko" and other operas, of the Tatar as opposed to the Russian in "Kitezh," and of the oriental in a good many pages of "Scheherazade" and "The Golden Cockerel"—always as a foil to the diatonic, folk-songish element that predominates in his music. It is easy to show that the exotic themes in "Scheherazade" (e.g., Ex. 27 in the first movement and the fanfare theme in the second) had their origin not in the music of the East but in the composer's own technical ingenuity. There is nothing as genuinely oriental as "Islamey" in the whole range of Rimsky-Korsakov's music.

It is not unreasonable to suppose that Balakirev's deeper sympathy with the East was due to heredity. He is said to have had Tatar blood in his veins, and Asiatic traits are discernible in his physiognomy. In Borodin's case this was even more marked. The energetic, pleasure-loving Georgian in him (he was a true Russian only on his mother's side) was generally predominant. Like Balakirev, Borodin betrays a natural leaning to the arabesque in many of his melodic lines, a type of free arabesque quite different from Rimsky-Korsakov's neat, symmetrical patterns. Borodin's frequent grace-notes, which are not mere ornaments but essential parts of the melodic line (as is often proved in the course of devlopment), are likewise symptomatic of the oriental tendency to elaboration of pure line. The quasi-eastern element in the music associated with the Polovtsi in "Prince

Igor" is, of course, intentional, like the character of the cor anglais melody of "In Central Asia." That is in the tradition—the oriental introduced as contrast to the Slavonic. But in movements like the Andante of the E flat Symphony and the favourite Nocturne from the D major Quartet the floridness of line seems to be quite spontaneous. Such cases of oriental influence on the essential texture of Russian music are extremely rare. To use a foolish cliché, they are the "exceptions that prove the rule." Broadly speaking, the oriental element in Russian music is purely external and decorative.

VII.—LISZT'S INFLUENCE ON THE "MIGHTY HANDFUL."

Hermann Laroche in his reminiscences of the young Tchaïkovsky* records that the composer "approached Liszt with hesitation and mistrust. During his student years, 'Orpheus' was the only one of Liszt's symphonic poems which attracted him. The 'Faust' Symphony he did not value till long afterwards. It is but fair to state that Liszt's symphonic poems, which enslaved a whole generation of Russian composers, exercised only an insignificant and ephemeral influence upon Tchaïkovsky."

So much for the twenty-year-old Tchaïkovsky of the early sixties. The mature Tchaïkovsky of twenty years later maintained precisely the same attitude: "Liszt's works leave me cold. They have more poetical intention than actual creative power, more colour than form—in short, in spite of being

---

* Quoted at considerable length in the English edition of "The Life and Letters of P. I. Tchaïkovsky."

externally effective, they are lacking in the deeper qualities. Liszt is just the opposite of Schumann, whose vast creative force is not in harmony with his colourless style of expression." (Letter to Mme. von Meck, November, 1881.)

In taking this view of Liszt, the young Tchaïkovsky was at first by no means at variance with his most important contemporaries in Russia, the fledglings of the Balakirev group. He was at one with them in admiring Glinka, Schumann and (of all composers) Henri Litolff. As for Wagner, the young Tchaïkovsky thought him less gifted than Serov, while the slightly older Borodin certainly voiced the opinions of the entire "handful" when he placed him below Meyerbeer. And during the first half of the sixties they would not have quarrelled about Liszt. The sixteen-year-old Rimsky-Korsakov heard "Prometheus" in 1860 and completely failed to understand it; he loved Beethoven, Glinka, and the "Midsummer Night's Dream" Overture, but "Prometheus" left on him a "strange, unclear impression." When he came into touch with Balakirev, Cui and Mussorgsky two or three years later, he found their opinion of Liszt even more decidedly unfavourable than his own. True, Liszt's work was "comparatively little known to them"—a frequent foundation of adverse musical judgments!—but what they did know they considered "musically perverse, fragmentary, even in the nature of caricature."

Liszt's Influence.

But whereas Liszt left Tchaïkovsky cold to the end of his life, the attitude of the Kuchkisti soon underwent a striking change. By 1866, Rimsky-Korsakov tells us in his "Memoirs," "the works of Liszt began to appear more and more often" in their circle, "particularly the 'Mephisto Waltz' and the 'Totentanz.'" The "Totentanz" was played for the first time in St. Petersburg by Mussorgsky's former piano-teacher, Anton Herke, at a concert of the Russian Music Society in March, 1866, Anton Rubinstein conducting. According to Rimsky-Korsakov: "Balakirev was indignant at Rubinstein's opinion of this piece. Rubinstein had called it a 'senseless piece of piano-pounding' or something like that. But although Rubinstein did not like Liszt, he afterwards changed his opinion of this work. I recollect that the 'Totentanz' also impressed me somewhat unpleasantly at the first hearing, but I soon recognised its value. On the other hand, the 'Mephisto Waltz' pleased me immensely. I got hold of the score and even learned to play it tolerably in an arrangement of my own." Balakirev conducted the "Waltz" at a Free School Symphony Concert in December, 1866,* and his entire circle was delighted with it.

---

* Rimsky-Korsakov mentions that at one of the rehearsals Lomakin, "blinking his eyes as if with pleasure" at the "Mephisto Waltz," "said to me: 'How Michael Ivanovich (Glinka) loved such music!' What did he mean by '*such* music'? Probably 'such sensuous, voluptuous' music."

The influence of Liszt's music, particularly the "Waltz" and "Totentanz" (paraphrase on the "Dies Iræ" for piano and orchestra), on the Kuchkisti now became so potent as almost to excuse, though not to justify, Laroche's sneer at their "enslavement" (but it was not, as he says, the symphonic poems that "enslaved" them). The first to succumb was Mussorgsky, who in 1867, confessedly under the influence of the "Totentanz," recast his earlier incidental music to Mengden's play, "The Witch," as an orchestral fantasia, "St. John's Night on the Bare Mountain."* It is impossible to say how much of the material of Mussorgsky's fantasia had existed previously, but it has more in common with Liszt's work than the macabre quality. It is even possible that the familiar:

of "St. John's Night" was unconsciously derived from one of Liszt's versions of the plainsong:

---

* The music subsequently underwent other metamorphoses and is now known to us, in a version completed and orchestrated by Rimsky-Korsakov, as "Night on the Bare Mountain."

Liszt's Influence. 85

Liszt's music also exercised a direct influence on another Russian orchestral piece, written in the summer of 1867, Rimsky-Korsakov's symphonic poem, "Sadko." According to the composer himself, the variations on Sadko's song and his *gusli* dance-melody, which become wilder and wilder as they depict the growing storm, "arose partly under the influence of certain passages in Liszt's 'Mephisto Waltz,'" while the earlier section (the feast in the submarine kingdom) contains echoes of the "Waltz" in both harmony and figuration. In a conversation with Yastrebtsev in 1893 the composer specified the actual points in the score—"the typical harmonies on pages 14, 20, 27-8 and 41-2 are likewise Lisztian, from that work of genius the 'Mephisto Waltz.'" The same unquestionable authority has also pointed out that "the introduction, depicting the tranquil swell of the sea, has the same harmonic and modulatory bases as the beginning of Liszt's 'Ce qu'on entend sur la montagne.'" The wave-motive, used again in the later opera on the same subject, is certainly worth comparing with a double-bass figure in Liszt's poem :

Finally, it seems not improbable that Rimsky-Korsakov was actually confirmed in his choice of the Sadko legend for orchestral treatment* by its similarity to the programme of the "Mephisto Waltz," in each case the raising of a storm of Dionysian excitement through the playing of a dæmonic musician. Rimsky-Korsakov also notes in his "Memoirs" the influence of Liszt's symphonic poems in general on the scoring of his "Antar" (written the year after "Sadko") and of the still closer influence of the "Hunnenschlacht" in particular on the second movement, which likewise depicts a battle.

"Antar" was no sooner finished than the Kuchkisti were introduced to a third piece by Liszt, which they found equally captivating. This was

---

* Originally suggested to Balakirev by Stassov in 1861.

"Der nächtliche Zug," the first Episode from Lenau's "Faust," heard for the first time in Russia when Balakirev conducted both the Episodes (the other, of course, being the "Waltz") at a concert of the Russian Music Society early in 1869. (Carl Tausig, to whom the "Episodes" are dedicated, is said to have first heard them at this concert.) Borodin, deputising for Cui as critic of the "Petersburg Vedomosti," wrote enthusiastically about both pieces. And it was these three works, the two "Faust" Episodes and the "Totentanz," still almost unknown to the average English musician, which principally—indeed, almost exclusively—fascinated the young Russian nationalists. They accepted the rest of Liszt's works only with reservations. Balakirev, for instance, admired the "marvellously motivated" form of "Les Préludes," "in which each idea flows naturally from the other," but he was keenly alive to the "cheapness" and "emptiness" of the opening of the storm episode and to the "extreme badness" of the love-theme on the horns "which sounds rather like 'Semiramide.'"

A quarter of a century later Rimsky-Korsakov was still of much the same opinion. He told Yastrebtsev in 1893 that he considered Liszt's compositions in general "too drawn out" and that he did not care for "Mazeppa," "Tasso" and the "Faust" Symphony. But he still valued above all the rest of Liszt's compositions the "Mephisto

Waltz" and "Der nächtliche Zug" ("with the exception of one thoroughly weak passage" in the latter). He also liked the second part of the "Offertorium" and the "Magnificat" in the "Dante" Symphony, "St. Elisabeth" (except the Crusaders' March and one or two other passages), and of the symphonic poems, the "Hunnenschlacht," "Les Préludes," "Ce qu'on entend sur la montagne" ("although the latter is too long"), "Hungaria" ("also very long!") and "Orpheus." In "Ideale," he considered that Liszt had attempted to go beyond the limits of possibility in programme-music.

It would not be difficult to find a number of passages, in addition to those already pointed out, where one or another of the "mighty handful" has evidently taken a direct hint from Liszt: for instance, Mussorgsky's tuning-up on the open strings which introduces the well-known gopak in his "Fair of Sorochintsy" probably suggested by the opening of the "Mephisto Waltz" or the tramp of Borodin's camels in "In Central Asia" for which he was obviously indebted to the passage in "Der nächtliche Zug" where Liszt suggests the leisurely gait of Faust's horse:

But Liszt's influence penetrated deeper than this into the musical style of the Russian nationalists. With Glinka and Berlioz, he was their master in orchestration. Berlioz naturally fascinated them and they all learned something of the secret of Glinka's delicate, transparent brilliance, but the rich sonority of their orchestral writing during the seventies and eighties approximates most nearly to Liszt's. They caught the timbre of his clear, bold, rich colouring in the tutti; they were charmed by his employment of bright primary colours, both of solo instruments and of instrumental groups; and they evidently noted his effective, if rather vulgar, use of the harp. Balakirev's exploitation, even development, of Lisztian piano technique in "Islamey" may be allowed to speak for itself. Harmonically and melodically the debt is equally great. Rimsky-Korsakov most probably learned from the "Faust" Symphony the expressive possibilities of the augmented triad, of which he became so fond; and on his own confession it was Liszt's employment of plain-song melodies (e.g., "Dies iræ" in the "Totentanz," "Pange lingua" in "Der nächtliche Zug," etc.) which first opened his eyes to the possibilities of the long-disused modes as alternatives to the conventional major and minor, a resource of which he availed himself in nearly all his works from "Snow Maiden" onwards. The progression of major triads on a descending whole-tone scale in the "Magnificat" of the "Dante"

Symphony obviously fascinated him too; the influence of this passage is apparent in many of his works (e.g., the chords at the opening of "Christmas Eve"). Curiously enough, it is not impossible that Liszt himself got the idea from Glinka's "Ruslan."

Rimsky-Korsakov, if not his comrades, also thoroughly absorbed into his musical system one of Liszt's least admirable characteristics, his trick of constructing music sectionally by the bare repetition (in different keys) of small, self-contained blocks of sound, skilfully dovetailed—a method of manufacturing music even more mechanical than the "bogus development" taught by professors of composition, against which Ernest Newman continually doth rage.

VIII.—THE COLLECTIVE "MLADA."

Early in 1872,* S. A. Gedeonov, archæologist and director of the Imperial Theatres and the Hermitage Palace Art Gallery in Petersburg, approached Vladimir Stassov with an unusual request. He wished to know whether four of Stassov's composer friends—Cui, Mussorgsky, Rimsky-Korsakov and Borodin—would care to collaborate in the composition of a great spectacular opera-ballet in four acts, "Mlada," devised by Gedeonov himself to exploit the scenic resources of the Maryinsky Theatre. He had concocted a sort of Drury Lane scenario, in which melodrama was curiously mingled with folk-lore and archæology, and fantasy with pageantry and dancing. The actual libretto was to be written by V. A. Krïlov, a dramatic hack not to be confused with the author of the celebrated "Fables," and the generous proportion of ballet

* Rimsky-Korsakov in his "Memoirs," wrongly places the event in the winter of 1870-1.

music by Minkus, the official ballet composer attached to the Imperial Theatres. The rest of the music was to be shared by the four Kuchkisti, and Gedeonov stipulated that, to prevent the piece being dragged out to an intolerable length, their contributions must be as concise as possible. All things considered, Stassov felt certain that they would refuse, and he was at first unwilling even to broach the subject to them.* But only one of the four, Cui, had so far had the satisfaction of seeing his work on the stage; Mussorgsky had had his first draft of "Boris" rejected by the directorate of the Imperial Theatres; Rimsky-Korsakov had just completed his "Pskovityanka" ("Ivan the Terrible"), but was having difficulties with the censorship over the libretto; while Borodin had so far done nothing but accumulate sketches for operas. The temptation of practically unlimited musical and scenic resources was too much for them, and they accepted the situation eagerly.

The first act was allotted to Cui, by common consent the "most dramatic" of the group, and the fourth to Borodin, while the two middle acts were rather curiously divided between Rimsky-Korsakov and Mussorgsky, an arrangement facilitated

---

* According to his own account in his "Borodin." Why, in the face of this definite statement, Rimsky-Korsakov (faithfully echoed by Oskar von Riesemann in his "Mussorgski") should have thought it possible that the idea of "Mlada" actually originated with Stassov, seems quite incomprehensible.

by the fact that they were sharing rooms that winter. According to their usual custom they all, except perhaps Cui, turned to account unused sketches made for other purposes. Borodin with his usual thoroughness—he was always rather like the man who blacked himself all over to play Othello—read Sreznevsky on old Slavonic religious beliefs and customs. And during March and April they all worked energetically. Cui's share was finished, Borodin's nearly, but the other two collaborators lagged. Already at the end of March, Mussorgsky was in a state of moral revolt against the idiotic libretto, the conditions insisted on by Gedeonov, and the general "prostitution" of the talents of the four collaborators, while Rimsky-Korsakov was held up, he says, by "the insufficiently worked-out scenario." And then came a crushing blow. It was found that Gedeonov had been too ambitious, and his ten thousand ruble production had to be abandoned.* Cui kept his first act intact, except for some material from the conjuration scene transferred to "Angelo" (1876), and published it as recently as 1911, "in memory of my dear comrades." But the other three, frugal as ever, simply re-adapted what they had written and used it in other works, though not before a performance of the

---

* Von Riesemann in his "Mussorgski," blindly accepts Rimsky-Korsakov's statement (in his "Memoirs") that "Gedeonov left his post as director of the Imperial Theatres and disappeared from the scene." Gedeonov did not resign till 1875.

whole of the completed parts had been given (with piano) at Cui's house on May 1. There was a sequel in 1889, when a chance remark of Lyadov's gave Rimsky-Korsakov the idea of tackling "Mlada" again, single-handed. He did so, after filling out and largely re-writing the Krïlov libretto, and the work, one of his most interesting scores, was completed in 1891 and produced the following year.

These facts have always been known, if not quite accurately, to students of Russian music. But the recent publication of Mussorgsky's contributions, with study of not yet translated sources, makes it possible to attempt a reconstruction in outline of practically the whole of the music of this very curious work.

Cui's first act, not unfairly representative of his rather pallid talent, is of special interest, since it preserves the original libretto and enables us to study the type of modification made by Rimsky-Korsakov twenty years later. There is no overture, but a prelude of fifty-six bars very typical of Cui's short-winded and anæmic lyrical style, with the slightest possible flavour of folk-song:

The Collective "Mlada." 95

(As usual, we hardly need the testimony of Cui's own confession to Tchaïkovsky that he always composed at the piano.)

The curtain rises on an open hall in the palace of Mstivoy, Prince of Retra, a ninth century city of the Polabian* or Baltic Slavs. Mstivoy (baritone) is on his throne, surrounded by his guards. His daughter, Voyslava (soprano) sits at her spinning wheel, while her maidens weave garlands for the approaching Festival of Kunava.† As they weave, they sing a weakly lyrical chorus partly based on Example 37; and then Voyslava breaks into a short mournful *arioso*, roughly interrupted by her father, who asks what is the matter with her. Mstivoy sings in Dargomïzhskian "melodic recitative," the type of operatic declamation which the Kuchkisti considered theoretically ideal, but which Cui's more gifted colleagues honoured with admiration rather than imitation. He takes the opportunity to remind his daughter, of what she knows only too well, of their joint crime on which the action, such as it is, hinges. Mstivoy is determined by motives of ambition to marry his daughter to Yaromir, Prince of Arkon, with whom she is passionately in love. But Yaromir had been betrothed to her friend, the Princess Mlada, and Voyslava at

---

* Laba = the Elbe.

† Rimsky-Korsakov changed the name of this festival, celebrating the summer solstice, to the more usual Christian form, "Kupala," i.e., the Eve of John the Baptist's Day.

her father's command has murdered Mlada with a poisoned ring during the wedding ceremony. However, the crime has not been discovered, and Yaromir is about to console himself with Voyslava. Mstivoy, having thus enlightened the audience, goes out and Voyslava renews her lamentations, reproaching Lada, the goddess of love and beauty, for abandoning her. Her old nurse, Svyatokhna (mezzo-soprano), having induced her to send the girls away—they go out singing a snatch of the prelude music—then tells her that it is useless to call on Lada; she must appeal to Morena, the death goddess.

There is some very Dargomïzhskian "modernism" in the orchestra both at this point and later, when Voyslava, after some hesitation, finally dedicates herself to the evil goddess:

38 *p* Pedal D

Subterranean thunder is heard—orchestrally painted with great restraint; darkness covers the stage; and Svyatokhna reveals that she herself is Morena, whose form she now assumes. She touches the Princess on the neck, where a bleeding wound appears—in Korsakov's version a purple flame springs from her head—and, having thus branded her new servant, vanishes.

Voyslava has barely time to pull herself together when Yaromir's hunting horns are heard. Mstivoy, the guards and girls reappear, and Yaromir (tenor) and his hunters enter with a boar's head which he offers to Voyslava (and for which she thanks him) to music of extraordinary banality. Cui's deference to Gedeonov's stipulation for brevity as contrasted with Korsakov's expansiveness when he had a free hand, is very noticeable in this episode: the chorus of greeting to Yaromir consists of merely eight bars in Cui's version as compared with Korsakov's sixty. And Korsakov at this point also inserted a long trio, as well as a ballet (the *redova* sometimes heard as a concert piece), with which no doubt Minkus was to have been entrusted in the original version. Cui gives Mstivoy and his daughter a mere eighteen bars of "melodic recitative" and allows them to withdraw again in rather impolite haste, leaving their guest alone with his thoughts.

The scene which follows is musically the best part of Cui's contribution. At first, Yaromir's mind follows Voyslava, though his "heart cannot forget Mlada." He becomes drowsy and the voices of an invisible chorus tell him to "Sleep, young knight, sleep to learn what you must know," for Lada is watching over his destiny. (Korsakov makes the goddess herself appear at this point.) In his first dream, Yaromir sees himself with Mlada as in the past, and his first declaration of love to her; in the second, his marriage ceremony and Voyslava's crime. He awakes in horror—and for once Cui's treatment of the situation compares favourably with Korsakov's—refusing to believe Voyslava's guilt and convinced that the vision was sent by the powers of darkness. He sings another feebly melodious aria to his lost Mlada, and then the people troop in again as purposelessly as ever. The act ends with a vigorous hunting chorus, much more "national" in flavour than anything which has preceded it. At the very end, Yaromir's characteristic fanfare (hardly a leitmotive) is woven into the orchestral accompaniment, and the act ends brilliantly and effectively.

So much for Cui's contribution, though in at least one respect the score published in 1911 differs from the true 1872 version. According to Yastrebtsev* the original music of the second dream, the wedding in the Temple of Svyatovid, was based on a melody by Rimsky-Korsakov:

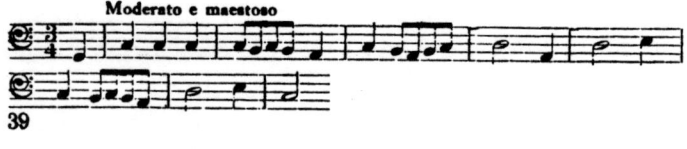

---

* "My Recollections of Rimsky-Korsakov" (entry of December 8, 1893).

which served as a "priests'" theme throughout the opera. Gedeonov's project having fallen through, Korsakov used this melody in 1875 in the *Andante* of his String Quartet in F, Op. 12, and later, when he took up "Mlada" afresh, restored it to its original place in the second dream episode. Consequently, Cui seems to have felt it necessary to write fresh music of his own for this passage.

If there is little genuine drama in Act I, there is even less in Acts II and III, which consist almost entirely of pageantry and fantastic ballet scenes. Act II opens with a crowded market scene before the Temple of Radegast in Retra; Mstivoy, Yaromir, and the other Polabian princes come to consult the auguries; and there is a scene of divination by the sacred horses—all, except the divination, composed by Mussorgsky. Then come dances by the foreign visitors, Minkus's share; and the act ends with the celebration of the festival of Kupala. The customary midsummer eve fires are lighted, and the young people join in a choral dance, composed by Rimsky-Korsakov, in which each young man kisses his partner. Voyslava and Yaromir dance with the rest, but each time that he is about to kiss her the shade of Mlada appears and separates them. The first part of Act III also fell to Rimsky-Korsakov's share. The scene is now Mount Triglav; it is night, and the spirits of the dead fly hither and thither. Yaromir appears, following Mlada's beckoning shade. But the spirits are frightened away by subterranean thunder—here Mussorgsky took over the composition—and Chernobog appears in the form of a black he-goat, with the other infernal deities, to celebrate their obscene rites. Implored by Morena, Chernobog calls up a vision of Cleopatra to seduce and destroy Yaromir, but the prince is saved just in time by the cockcrow which announces dawn and the end of the reign of evil.

The collaboration of Mussorgsky and Rimsky-Korsakov in the second act of "Mlada" (for the third hardly exists at all) produced some extremely interesting music. Mussorgsky's recently published market scene (156 bars sketched out for chorus and piano duet) opens with a prelude in the mixolydian mode:

After some unaccompanied choral phrases, invoking the help and protection of Radegast, comes a crowd scene full of genuine life, with naturalistic and unconventional handling of the chorus in the manner (if not on the level) of the crowd scenes in "Boris." The principal theme of this "market" music:

was afterwards used by Mussorgsky in the introduction and fair scene of his "Fair of Sorochintsy" (1876-7). Presently a quarrel breaks out between the Polabians and the traders of Novgorod, and a scene of fisticuffs ensues. In his setting of 1891, Rimsky-Korsakov evaded the actual fight scene and created a point of repose by introducing a singer, Lumir, who comes between the two parties and inflames both sides against the Christian Teutons. But Mussorgsky, ever attracted by opportunities for naturalistic experiment, planned an elaborate choral scene with three separate choruses—the women, the Polabians and the men of Novgorod—each in four parts. Unfortunately, it was never written. We have only forty-eight bars of four-hand piano accompaniment, from which, however, it is evident that Mussorgsky intended to use here the material of a chorus originally composed as part of the music to Sophocles's "Œdipus" in 1860-1, and which he had already tried to turn to account in his projected "Salammbo" opera (1863-6).*

---

* The chorus was published posthumously in 1883 by Rimsky-Korsakov.

The princes now enter to consult the omens. Their processional march, completed in piano duet form, with chorus parts and full indications of the intended scoring, was evidently the first number composed by Mussorgsky, for the manuscript is dated February 26, 1872. After an introduction based on a rhythmical figure on trumpets behind the scenes, with answering phrases in the orchestra, comes the march proper (entry of the guards and other attendants), a series of simple variations on a Russian folk-song.* The treatment is on the lines of Glinka's "Kamarinskaya," the melody being repeated unchanged against constantly varying backgrounds. At the trio of the march, the priests enter; the time changes to 3-4 and the theme is Ex. 39 (Mussorgsky acknowledged in a note on the manuscript that "the theme is Rimsky-Korsakov's.") The original march theme is then resumed, but treated rather differently, and built up to a climax, the folk-tune being thundered out in notes of double time-value when the princes themselves appear.†

---

* A hauling song from the Nizhny-Novgorod government, No. 6 in Balakirev's collection of folk-songs. Tchaïkovsky has used the same melody in the introduction to the finale of his String Serenade, Op. 48.

† On the strength of Rimsky-Korsakov's assertion, it is often stated that Mussorgsky used this "March of the Princes" for his "March with Trio alla turca," the accompaniment to a projected living picture, "The Taking of Kars," in 1880, simply substituting a fresh trio based on a Kurdish folk-tune for the original

The Collective "Mlada." 103

At the end of the march the chief priest calls for silence and the sacred horses are brought in, the "priests'" theme being modified so as to suggest the trampling of the horses :

an effect, obviously suggested by Liszt (cf. Ex. 36), which Rimsky-Korsakov recollected at the same point in his 1889 setting. The manuscript ends with eight bars in Rimsky-Korsakov's writing: the beginning of the chorus sung by the hushed people as the horses are led over the lances to determine the omens. The fragment consists simply of the priests' theme sung in octaves by tenors and basses with orchestra in unison.

Act II ends with the choral dance celebrating the festival of Kupala, composed by Rimsky-Korsakov, and subsequently used for the *khorovod* of the rusalkas in the last act of his " May Night " :

---

one. But there are textual differences, possibly due to Korsakov's "editing" in the later version of the march, which also has the first section exactly repeated instead of being built up to a climax as in the "Mlada" version. The original form of the march is much the better piece of work.

When Korsakov took up "Mlada" again, he expressed regret that he had not saved this melody for its original purpose. As a matter of fact, there is a distinct echo of the old music in the new:

Of Korsakov's music to Act III nothing has been published, though Andrey Rimsky-Korsakov in a footnote to the fourth (Russian) edition of his father's "Memoirs," says that a pianoforte arrangement of the introduction to Act III (night on Mount Triglav, and the flight of the shades of the dead) is preserved among his father's papers, and adds that "musically it offers foretastes of certain ideas in future operas—the queen of the rusalkas in 'May Night,' and the will-o'-the-wisps in 'Snegurochka.'" Although the composer himself always admitted that the harmonic basis of the "will-o'-the-wisps" theme:

The Collective "Mlada." 105

originated in "Mlada," he denied to Yastrebtsev (December 17, 1893) that the music itself was taken from the earlier work and "asserted that the music written *then*, and from which the 'will-o'-the-wisps' afterwards partly developed, was in his opinion so incongruous that he altogether rejected the episode as a mere string of extremely dissonant harmonies." On the same occasion Yastrebtsev learned that Mizgir's pleading phrase:

in "Snegurochka," also originated in the earlier work, being associated with Mlada herself.

The appearance of Chernobog and the other evil deities provided an opportunity for a fresh appearance of that unhappy ghost, "Night on the Bare Mountain," which haunted Mussorgsky for years, and was laid at last after his death (not without much trouble) by Rimsky-Korsakov in the form in which we know it. It seems to have been originally conceived as part of the music to Mengden's play, "The Witch"; later, it had been turned into a fantasia for piano and orchestra* in the manner of Liszt's "Totentanz"; now it went into the third act of "Mlada"; and when Mussorgsky died he left it as part of his unfinished "Fair of Sorochintsy." But in each form its function was the same. It always depicted a witches' sabbath. For its inclusion in "Mlada," Mussorgsky added choral parts to the music. In a letter to Stassov (March 31, 1872), he complains bitterly of having to set to music nonsense like "Sagana, chukh!" (that is, "demon language" in the manner of Berlioz's "Faust"); but the manuscript of this version is not yet published. As for the "Cleopatra" episode, one of the most effective passages in Rimsky-Korsakov's "Mlada," since I can find no mention of it in connection with the work of 1872, I conjecture that it was merely verbally discussed at this time by Gedeonov and Krïlov—or was perhaps entirely devised by Korsakov himself later.

In setting the fourth act, Borodin enjoyed the advantage of a rather less amorphous scenario. After another big choral scene before the temple of Radegast (or possibly, in the original libretto, *in*

---

* As Rimsky-Korsakov's bare statement is the only evidence that the piano was included, and as Mussorgsky himself does not mention it in his own detailed discussions of the work, I am inclined to think that Korsakov's memory was again at fault. Calvocoressi agrees with me that the "fantasia" was probably for orchestra only.

the temple), Yaromir appears and pours out his troubles to the chief priest, who tells him to wait alone before the temple at night, when the spirits of his ancestors will appear and advise him. Doing so, the prince receives the terse admonition: "Voyslava poisoned Mlada; avenge her!" Voyslava opportunely appears at this very moment and, after a duet in which she pleads her love as an excuse, Yaromir takes her by the hair and stabs her. Dying, she calls on Morena to avenge her in turn. The death-goddess appears and carries off the body of her dedicated slave; and, at her command, a storm rises, the temple of Radegast is destroyed by an earthquake, and the waters of Lake Dolin rise and inundate the whole town. But Gedeonov was still able to achieve the crowning banality of a happy ending. As the storm dies down, and the sun rises over the waste of water, a rainbow appears; the figures of Mlada and Yaromir are seen embracing in the sky; and the beneficent deities, Perun-Radegast, Lel, Lada, and the rest, advance on the clouds* and bless the lovers.

Borodin's contribution to the communal work was in the opinion of his three collaborators the best of all. And they were undoubtedly right. But apart from its intrinsic value, the music is specially interesting for its intimate connection with that of

---

* Rimsky-Korsakov found in 1892 that an actual procession was impracticable, and, much to his disgust, was obliged to substitute a *tableau vivant*.

"Prince Igor." Borodin had for some time lost interest in "Igor," and when the "Mlada" commission presented itself, he quickly turned to account such material as he had accumulated for the other opera. Thus the theme of Yaroslavna's dream, part of her *arioso* in the first act of "Igor," and the first thing Borodin wrote for it (September, 1869):

47

was used as a sort of "Yaromir" motif. Yaromir himself sang it in his scene with the chief priest. Naturally, when "Mlada" was dropped, and "Igor" resumed, this material was restored to its original place. Not only that, but practically all the fresh music composed for "Mlada" was transferred as well: most of it to form the prologue which had not been included in the original scheme of "Igor." So from the accounts of Stassov, Yastrebtsev, and others, we can practically reconstruct Act IV of "Mlada" from the materials of "Igor." A facsimile in Stassov's "Borodin" of the sketch (dated March 5, 1872) of the opening temple scene, with the choruses of priests and people:

48

shows that this was the origin of the chorus in the prologue which answers Igor's call to arms. The sacred horns of the priests of Radegast (bar one of Ex. 48) simply became Igor's signal trumpets! But a melody which appears in the last two bars of the example given in Stassov was taken from this context and transferred to the *opening* chorus in "Igor." The theme of the chief priest became the orchestral introduction to the prologue, and the music accompanying the appearance of Yaromir's ancestors was transferred note for note to the episode of the eclipse.

The duet between Voyslava and Yaromir* served later as the basis for the trio (Igor, his son, and Konchakovna) in Act III, where the Polovtsian chieftain's daughter tries to keep her lover from joining his father in flight. The principal theme is familiar from its appearance in the "Igor" overture:

49

However, the bulk of the remainder of the "Mlada" music (the appearance of Morena, the flood and storm:

---

* In which, as may be seen from the autograph preserved in the Leningrad Public Library, Mussorgsky also had a hand. This manuscript is dated March 12, 1872, and marked with the duration of the piece, "4 minutes."

50

from which Rimsky-Korsakov appears to have taken some useful hints for his own inundation, and the final apotheosis):

51

was left untouched, though Borodin did toy for a while with the idea of introducing a "flood" intermezzo in "Igor."* (According to legend, the River Don overflowed its banks to hinder the Polovtsi in their pursuit.) Incidentally, it was the playing over of the draft of this music in 1889, on the second anniversary of the composer's death, which occasioned Lyadov's suggestion to Rimsky-Kor-

---

* See note on page 163.

sakov, and so led the latter to take up the subject afresh. And in the following year Korsakov scored his dead friend's finale, and published it through Belaïev as a concert piece for orchestra only, with a brief explanatory programme. Only one episode of the finale, the chorus accompanying the procession of gods, was omitted from this concert version, since Borodin had himself transferred it to the final scene of "Igor" (the presentation of bread and salt to the returned prince.)

With the exception of the temple scene and love duet, the autographs of all Borodin's numbers are dated "April 14th, 1872," evidently the day on which they were written down or on which the writing down was finished, not the date of actual composition. With characteristic thoroughness, the composer marked each piece with its duration: appearance of Morena, one minute; flood, storm and destruction of the temple, one and a half minutes; appearance of Mlada, half a minute; apotheosis, one and a half minutes.

* * *

"Mlada" nearly had an epilogue. A year or two before, Mussorgsky had written a song, "The Peepshow," in which four conservative musicians—Zaremba, the director of the Petersburg Conservatoire; Theophil Tolstoy, the critic; and the two critic-composers, Serov and Famintsyn—were musically caricatured, and shown joining in a final hymn to a pseudo "Euterpe" (the Grand Duchess Helena Pavlovna, patroness of the Imperial Russian Music Society). Now, disappointed with "Mlada," and a little ashamed at the haste with which they had all accepted this "degrading" commission, Rimsky-Korsakov suggested that Mussorgsky should write a second "Peepshow," this time loosing the arrows of his satire against the four fallen angels of the Kuchka (including himself, of course), with Gedeonov as their patron deity. Mussorgsky accepted the suggestion with enthusiasm, but for some reason, perhaps preoccupation with the new idea of "Khovanshchina," this companion piece to "The Peepshow," was never written. It is a pity, for the world's song literature is not very rich in satire.

IX.—RIMSKY-KORSAKOV'S "MLADA."

We must remember that when, on Lyadov's suggestion, Rimsky-Korsakov decided in 1889 to tackle the old libretto afresh, the intervening seventeen years had brought many changes both to Rimsky-Korsakov personally, and to the general musical situation in Russia. Instead of maturing gradually and normally, his talent had passed through more than one crisis deeply affecting its means of expression, while leaving its essential nature quite untouched. The twenty-eight year old Korsakov of 1872 was still, in spite of his recent extraordinary appointment as professor of free composition at the Petersburg Conservatoire,* a mere gifted amateur who, on the strength of natural artistic instinct and an exceptional sense of orchestral colour, had (under Balakirev's guidance) written several piquant orchestral pieces, and an as yet unproduced opera: the first version of "Pskovityanka."

---

* A professor who, on his own confession, "could not have harmonised a chorale properly, had never written a single counterpoint exercise in my life, and didn't even know the names of the augmented and diminished intervals or of the chords, other than the tonic triad and the dominant and diminished sevenths."

The professorial appointment had an unforeseen consequence. Korsakov was obliged to start his musical education again from the beginning, and during the first half of the seventies, the former musical revolutionary was transformed into an academic conservative, almost into a mere pedant. He was rescued from that dismal fate by editorial work—harmonising folk-song collections and editing Glinka's operas—and the end of that decade saw the appearance of the delightful results of these two influences, the operas, "May Night" and "Snegurochka" ("Snow Maiden"). The period 1881-88 was once again deplorably barren. Mussorgsky and Borodin died, and Korsakov busied himself with the completion and orchestration of their unfinished works. He was occupied as well with academic work, and his position in the Russian musical world was now firmly established. About 1888 he produced in a group his three most famous orchestral works, the "Spanish Capriccio," "Scheherazade," and the "Easter" Overture. And then surprisingly enough came another deluge: Wagnerism.

Wagner had been one of the *bêtes noires* of the "mighty handful," in spite of their admiration for Liszt. Borodin had said that the "Meistersinger" Overture "might be taken for the prelude to some utterly uninspired oratorio, depicting the downfall of the walls of Jericho!" Certainly, the first Petersburg performance of the "Ring" in the winter of 1888-9, shook the rather jerry-built walls of Korsakov's self-confidence. Incomparably brilliant as his own orchestral technique had become, he was completely captivated by Wagner's. He studied it intensively, and absorbed many of its elements into his own style. Not only that, but he now definitely embarked on a career as an opera composer, producing a fresh work every year or so, and writing hardly anything but for the theatre. "Mlada" was the first product of this new period of activity, the period which was to produce such masterpieces as "Sadko," "Saltan," "Kitezh" and the "Cockerel."

The scenario of "Mlada," with its spectacle, its gods, its rainbow, its final inundation, and its hero temporarily in love with the wrong woman, has accidental points of resemblance to the "Ring" which possibly gave it a new, factitious attractiveness in Korsakov's eyes. He had evidently come under the spell not only of Wagner's orchestra, but of Wagner's steam-curtains. The intoxication of scoring for an orchestra of Wagnerian dimensions urged him to reckless extravagance in other respects. "The opera-ballet 'Mlada' demands a large stage and complicated scenic apparatus," begins the preface to the score. He asks for a large chorus (divisible into small groups), a large *corps de ballet*, and, in addition to the already very big orchestra, a number of special instruments (pan-pipes, etc.) for the "Cleopatra" scene. For the market scene in Act II, ten secondary soloists are necessary, and "the composer cannot permit the substitution of choral groups for these additional soloists." That gives the tone of the whole preface. Exasperated by cuts and alterations in the production of his earlier operas, the composer demanded that "Mlada" should be given exactly as he wanted it, or not at all. Tartly pointing out that "the length of it (about two-and-a-half hours of music) cannot tire anyone," he goes on to insist that there shall be no abbreviations. All entries, exits, lighting effects, and so on, must coincide exactly with the corresponding bars in the music, as many of these stage directions "have significance *only in connection with the music.*" The timing of the music in the transformation scenes is indicated precisely in seconds. Rather amusingly, however. Korsakov had no sooner finished the third act—the first to be orchestrated—of this work so intimately related to stage-effect (the act perhaps *most* intimately so related) than he had it performed as a concert piece for tenor solo, chorus, and orchestra! In fact, it was actually given twice in this way before the first performance of the opera at the Maryinsky Theatre, Petersburg, on October 20 November 1, 1892. And then, after all, the composer found himself obliged to consent to considerable cuts in the final chorus!

As a stage-work "Mlada" remains badly handicapped by the libretto. The original libretto was devised for spectacle only and, despite his drastic textual alterations, Korsakov could make very little of it. As he confessed, he "simply didn't know how to develop" the "laconic shortness" of the text. Unlike Wagner, he had no gift for the invention of metaphysical disquisitions which could be put in the mouths of his characters when the action was at a standstill. Without action he found it next to impossible to invent anything for them to say, and the old-fashioned set aria, with its verbal repetitions, which got over that difficulty in the old days, was excluded by the operatic convention he had chosen to adopt. To fill out the proportions of the work he could only inflate the spectacular and picturesque episodes, just as later in re-writing Mussorgsky's "Boris" he inserted thirty-two extra bars of processional music in the coronation scene. But these episodes are handled so well, provided with music as colourful as almost any he ever wrote, that one is almost induced to overlook the pointlessness of it all. The hopelessly undramatic second act—with its market-scene (prototype of the still finer harbour-scene in "Sadko"); Lumir's modal song, with *gusli* and *gudok* accompaniment (a worthy link in the chain of such songs which runs through nearly all Korsakov's operas); the brilliantly orchestrated procession of the princes; the scene of divination by horses; the Lithuanian and Indian dances; and the final choral round—is simply a disconnected series of charming and characteristically Korsakovian pieces, of which only the last has anything to do with the plot. Wagnerism or no Wagnerism, then, "Mlada" is not even the ghost of a music-drama; and later, comparing it with its successors, "Christmas Eve" and "Sadko," the composer himself admitted that "the unsatisfactory development of the dramatic action injures the work, and the description of old customs and the fantastic element come too prominently to the fore." (Actually, of course, the plot is only an excuse for putting these on the stage.) And he considered "Mlada" decidedly inferior to "Snegurochka." There he was right. With all its charming music, it lacks the limpid freshness of the earlier work without attaining the breadth of handling, the depth of national feeling, and the exuberant fantasy of "Sadko." And there is throughout a queer hotch-potch of styles: Lisztian (arrival of Yaromir in Act I, and much of the fantastic music of Act III); Wagnerian (the beginning and end of Act III, the chorus of Spirits of Light in the dream scene, and bits of dialogue in other parts); Balakirevian (the Cleopatra scene); folk-songish (opening chorus of Act I and the choral dance which ends Act II); even Chopinesque (the *redova* in Act I), together, of course, with much that could have been written by no one but Korsakov himself.

One of the most interesting secondary features of "Mlada" is the introduction of the oriental element, which had hitherto been practically confined to two or three of Korsakov's symphonic works : the early "Serbian Fantasia," "Antar," and "Scheherazade." It was probably the success of the last which prompted the injection into "Mlada" of an ingredient by no means demanded by the subject. Indeed, the cry of the Moorish merchant in the market scene (prototype of the all-too-celebrated, and musically more expansive, Hindu merchant in the corresponding scene of "Sadko"), with its accompaniment of thrummed strings :

52

is obviously a by-product of the cadenzas in the second movement of "Scheherazade." There are Indians also in "Mlada," though what grounds Korsakov had* for bringing Indian merchants to the Baltic in the ninth, tenth, or any other century would, I fancy, be difficult to establish. Their dance likewise recalls "Scheherazade" (third

---

* It is clear from Mussorgsky's setting of the market scene that the Moor was a later interpolation of Rimsky-Korsakov's own. So probably the Indians were, as well.

movement). It is a pleasant little bit of ballet-music, but bears about as much relation to genuine Hindu music as cocoa does to the coconut. But it is in the Cleopatra scene (which Balakirev considered "real music *à la* 'Tamara'") that Korsakov indulges most riotously in the oriental. It is a masterpiece of its kind, the only comparable passage being the end of the second act of "The Golden Cockerel" which is closely modelled on it. It is typical of Rimsky's rather casual, far from pedantic, attitude to orientalism that of the two genuine eastern tunes associated with the Egyptian queen, one is Persian and the other Caucasian:

53

modified from one collected by Balakirev, who held that Korsakov had spoiled it by flattening two of the C's in bar 4. The rest of the "oriental" material is absolutely spurious. For instance, the theme of the *tsevnitsy* (panpipes) played by the male slaves:

54

which sounds so genuinely exotic, is based not on some oriental scale, but on the artificial one of alternate tones and semitones invented by Rimsky-Korsakov himself.

Noteworthy, too, are the "symphonic pictures" ("Night on Mount Triglav," the flood and rainbow at the end, and so on) which from "Mlada" onward became a prominent feature of Rimsky-Korsakov's operas, and which mark the end of his attempts to write genuinely symphonic music for the concert-room. As with later operas ("Christmas Eve" and "Tsar Saltan") he published a concert suite from "Mlada," consisting of the Introduction (a tone-portrait of Mlada herself), the *redova* of Yaromir's hunters and the girls, the Lithuanian and Indian dances, and the brilliant Procession of the Princes—by no means the cream of the work. But if someone would give us concert performances (with chorus) of, say, the market scene or the Cleopatra scene—and if contraltos would occasionally give us Lumir's song—musicians in general would have reason to be grateful. And I, for one, would not clamour for a stage-production, even if such were a little more feasible than it is.

X.—"TSAR SALTAN."

What does one expect? It is a call to attention, "a sort of invitation to see and hear what is now going to be represented," as the composer said. It is precise and yet it has a flavour of the fantastic, or at least of the unexpected. But at the same time there is no enchantment in it. No magic casements fly open at its sounds. One remembers it, but one remembers it as a brilliant idea, not as an inspiration. It is the musical equivalent of an epigram rather than of a poet's thought. And so, to a certain extent, this fanfare which opens the prologue and each act of Rimsky-Korsakov's "Tsar Saltan" accurately symbolises not only the nature of this particular musical tale but the nature of Korsakov's gifts in general. One might go on and suggest that its sudden but matter-of-fact switchback between unexpected keys symbolises the intimate juxtaposition in his art of the real and the fantastic, or of the humorous and the poetic. Indeed, nothing is easier than to hear a great deal more in this fanfare than there is any justification for hearing, for after all it is only "a sort of invitation . . . a new and happily employed device for a fairy-tale opera," though he who said so should not have done—being the composer thereof. But it is not for nothing that it pervades the whole "legend" as a sort of motto-theme and, sung by the whole company, rounds it off at the end.

"Tsar Saltan" is not by any means Rimsky-Korsakov's greatest opera, but perhaps more than any of the others it contains all the most characteristic elements of his work with the minimum of alloy. It is almost *un*alloyed, in fact. Leaving out of account the altogether untypical operas, like "The Tsar's Bride" or "Servilia," even in his most characteristic operas ("Sadko," perhaps, excepted), those which could not possibly have been written by anyone but himself, the essential Korsakov is either not revealed completely or is mingled with some foreign element: the influence of Dargomïzhsky, or Glinka, or Wagner, or the Italians. It may be said that the oriental element is missing from "Tsar Saltan," but actually (as we have already seen) the oriental element in Rimsky-Korsakov's music is proportionately very small, seeming bigger only because it has chanced to catch the fancy of the public. As I have pointed out elsewhere,* Korsakov's special contribution to music is the evocation of "a fantastic world entirely his own, half-real, half-supernatural, a world as limited, as distinctive and as delightful as the worlds of the Grimms' fairy-tales or as Alice's Wonderland. It is a world in which the commonplace and matter-of-fact are inextricably confused with the fantastic, *naïveté* with sophistication, the romantic with the humorous, and beauty with absurdity." Its chief weakness is its emotion, which is too often commonplace and unconvincing in expression and mixes badly with the other elements. Yet without its touch the characters would remain mere puppets, making no demand on our sympathy. It cannot be said that this world was created by Rimsky-Korsakov. It was created in literature by Pushkin, and has its origin in the traditional tales and songs of the Russian people; it is no mere coincidence that "Tsar Saltan," the most perfect projection of this world, is based on a tale of Pushkin's. But Korsakov must be given all the credit of having invented music (one might almost say a type of music) that conjures up such a world to the imagination, even without the help of scenery and poetry. It is all make-believe. But we know that the composer regarded art itself as a

---

* "Masters of Russian Music." By M. D. Calvocoressi and Gerald Abraham.

splendid make-believe, and we know how that view of his offended Mussorgsky who sought in art truth first and all other things a long way after. But "Tsar Saltan" is genuine make-believe, the real thing. The composer is out to enjoy himself and there is no tongue in the cheek, as in "The Golden Cockerel," to spoil our pleasure. Although "Tsar Saltan" was written in 1899, nineteen years later than "Snegurochka," it belongs so nearly to the same mental world (and almost the same musical world) as to be a natural companion-piece. Not that Rimsky-Korsakov had kept unimaginatively to the same operatic formula for all those years. After "Snegurochka" he left opera alone for a whole decade and then, having heard the "Ring," wrote a trio of works bearing traces of Wagnerian influence—"Mlada" (1890), "Christmas Eve" (1894) and "Sadko" (1895). These were followed by two short "declamatory" works in the Dargomïzhsky-Mussorgsky tradition, "Mozart and Salieri" (1897) and "Vera Sheloga" (1898), and by that curious essay in Bizet's manner, "The Tsar's Bride" (1898). "Tsar Saltan" was therefore a return to an earlier style, though not a final return. Korsakov was to indulge in the still more erratic experiments of "Servilia," "Kashchey" and "Pan Voevoda" before he rounded off his career with the two characteristic masterpieces, "Kitezh" and "The Golden Cockerel."

The decision to base an opera on Pushkin's fantastic "Tale of Tsar Saltan, his son the mighty and famous hero, Guidon, and the beautiful Swan Princess" seems to have been taken quite suddenly. Korsakov and V. I. Belsky, the librettist of his later works, had discussed a number of subjects—"Kitezh" and Byron's "Heaven and Earth" among others—but not "Saltan." Then in the winter of 1898, this theme took the composer's fancy and with his literary collaborator he worked out a scenario. Belsky began the libretto in the spring, "using Pushkin's verses as much as possible and imitating their style in a masterly way"; Korsakov set to work on each scene as he received it; and by the end of the summer the whole opera was composed and the Prologue and First Act completely scored. The opera had its first performance at the Solodovnikov Theatre in Moscow on October 21-November 2, 1900. But before this the familiar orchestral suite of "Pictures from the Tale of Tsar Saltan" (i.e., the preludes to the first and second acts and the final scene) had been played at one of Belaïev's Russian Symphony Concerts.

Criticism naturally fastens on the obvious weakness of "Saltan" as a drama. In fact, there is hardly any genuinely dramatic element in it at all. The story, an interweaving of the Cinderella theme with that of Danaë and Perseus, richly and humorously embroidered *à la russe*, is merely a succession of fantastic happenings serving as a framework for music. But for Rimsky-Korsakov it was a nearly ideal framework. Inconstant in his operatic theories though he was, his best work was done under the conviction expressed in the prefatory notes to "Tsar Saltan," "Sadko" and "Kitezh," that "an opera is first and foremost a musical work." And Pushkin's version of this old folk-tale, many of its incidents formalised into a sort of ritual (in the manner of the Three Bears), provided him with a pretext for music far more congenial than he found in a genuine drama like "The Tsar's Bride."

Pushkin's sharply characterised puppets were well within the range of a composer who was seldom happy in finding music for a human being of flesh and blood. Neither the characters nor the situations in "Tsar Saltan" call for psychological subtlety or dramatic power. The emotions are conventional, as the emotions in fairy-tales usually are, and the spectator is not expected to share them. He watches the action through the wrong end of a telescope, as it were. But if the puppet-characters are too remote for us to sympathise with them, they are astonishingly lifelike, just as a good caricature is lifelike, and the music brings out their half-human, half-puppetlike characteristics with almost visual suggestiveness. The motive associated with the foolish Tsar, for instance, at once naïve and pompous, fussy and good-humoured :

suggests the jerky, precise movements of a marionette. There is the same humorous simplicity in much of the melodic quasi-recitative, where the music is the perfect equivalent of the quaint, childish, metrical pattern that Pushkin borrowed from Russian folk-poetry:

In his memoirs Korsakov tells us that he took pains to give the recitatives "a peculiar, naïve character suitable to a fairy-tale." And he has admirably succeeded.

In accordance with his usual practice, Rimsky-Korsakov mingled two musical styles in "Tsar Saltan," a relatively simple and diatonic style for the music associated with the more real characters (Saltan, Militrissa and the Sisters) and one more piquant and harmonically complicated for purely fantastic and dreamlike beings such as the Swan Princess. The leitmotive system is accepted wholeheartedly. And as usual the folk-song element plays an important part in the score.

But perhaps the most striking feature of "Tsar Saltan" is its formalised design. All that Rimsky-Korsakov usually demanded of an operatic subject was that it should provide a suitable skeleton for him to cover with musical flesh. And he found "Saltan" peculiarly congenial not only because of its fantastic content but on account of its *shape*. The tendency to reduce a story to a more or less symmetrical pattern is apparent in the fairy-tales of all countries; and this trait in the telling of "The Tale of Tsar Saltan" particularly appealed to Rimsky-Korsakov, for whom music was always essentially a matter of symmetrical pattern and who had always striven in his operas to impose purely musical shapes (equivalent to the old aria and rondo forms) on long dramatic scenes instead of following the dramatic development with a free symphonic tissue in Wagner's way.* He has given us masterly examples of this curiously formalised type of structure in the harbour scene of "Sadko" and the final scene of "Kitezh," but no other subject gave him such scope for it as "Saltan." This formalisation is noticeable at the very beginning, in the conversa-

---

* Though, as a matter of fact, recent research has demonstrated that Wagner himself paid far more attention to purely musical architecture than is commonly supposed.

tion of the sisters in the Prologue, and it is applied on a much larger scale in the first half of Act I. All the music of this scene, up to the appearance of the little Tsarevich Guidon, is moulded into a kind of gigantic rondo, with the lullaby of the Tsarevich's nurses behind the scenes as the principal subject and the songs of the Buffoon and the old Storyteller, with the entrances of the two Elder Sisters and Militrissa's replies to their offers of presents, as episodes. So we have:

Lullaby (C major).
Buffoon's song.
Entrance of the Eldest Sister.
Old Man's petition and dialogue with Buffoon.
Lullaby (B major).
First part of Old Man's tale.
Entrance of the Middle Sister.
Second part of Old Man's tale.
Lullaby (B flat major).

The same symmetry dominates the first part of the scene at Saltan's court, the entertainment of the sailors. And it is still more elaborately employed in the second part, when the sailors excite Saltan's curiosity by reciting the wonders of Ledenets. The Second Sailor tells how the wonderful city itself arose; the First of Guidon's marvellous squirrel which cracks golden nuts with emerald kernels; and the Third of the thirty-three heroes whom Guidon has at his command. After the description of each wonder the Tsar announces—to the same phrase, a variation of Ex. 56—his intention of going to see it for himself. Each wonder is scoffed at by the Eldest Sister, the Middle Sister and Barbarikha respectively, and each of these is stung in turn by the bumble-bee. And the actual appearance of the wonders in the last scene, each commented on in the same way by Saltan and Guidon, is treated on similar lines.

Whereas another composer might have felt himself hampered by all this, Korsakov finds in it the exact equivalent of his own natural musical style, in form as much as in content. His symphonic music does not unfold and develop from itself, generating its own life and motive power as it goes along. No music in the world has ever been more empty of *rhythm* in the broadest sense of that vague word. It is a mosaic, a delightful arrangement of little musical tiles (often exquisite in themselves). There is often no reason why they should be arranged in one way rather than another. As no form arises naturally from the content of this music, it has to be fitted into some conventional form, into some more or less disguised and modified symmetry. The shape of a formalised fairy-tale provides an ideal ground-plan for such music.

Rimsky-Korsakov's gift for visual suggestion has already been referred to. It was a power that came to him rather late in life and is seen at its best in "The Golden Cockerel." But "Saltan" is full of little scraps of tune or rhythm evoking to the mind's eye movements and gestures and thus sharply stamping an impression of the character on the imagination. The delightful characteristic theme of Saltan himself has already been quoted. Consider also the motives suggesting the petty malice of the sisters :

These themes make their effect by an almost visual vividness reminding one of Mussorgsky, who was a perfect master of this sort of suggestion (e.g., the scrivener in "Khovanshchina," the two Jews in the "Pictures from an Exhibition," and Shuisky in "Boris").

But whereas Mussorgsky uses this method to characterise only minor figures, in contrast with the elaborate psychological analysis of the chief protagonists, Rimsky-Korsakov has no other means than this of delineating even principal figures. (Ivan the Terrible in "Pskovityanka" and Grishka Kuterma in "Kitezh" are quite exceptional). Equally superficial and external is his nature tone-painting (e.g., the sea-picture of the Introduction to Act II of "Tsar Saltan," and the interlude depicting night and sunrise later in the same Act). Rimsky-Korsakov can neither express the moods of nature nor even suggest natural appearances to the mind's eye with anything like the precision of Wagner (the flowing Rhine or the flickering fire) nor as sharply and definitely as he himself can sometimes suggest a human character like his foolish Tsar. He again and again attempts tone-painting without having any real flair for it; he writes essentially abstract music congruent to the matter in hand. That is all. Possibly his character-sketching is no more; but there does seem to be a definite pantomimic element in it which is necessarily lacking in a painting of a scene. No doubt his tone-painting was precise enough to his own mind, particularly as he uses the same conventional figures to depict the same things in different works, for instance the "wave" motives in "Scheherazade" and "Tsar Saltan" respectively:

And it is clear that his faculty of definite key-association helped considerably to give precision to otherwise rather vague impressions. But unless we share the composer's vivid perception of the "dark, steely blueness" of B major and the "brightness and rosiness" of A major (and that is more than any composer has the right to expect) his musical painting of night and sunrise in "Tsar Saltan" will necessarily be less realistic to us than it was to him. Unless we know his work fairly intimately we shall not even be aware of the coincidence that he uses the same keys for night and sunrise in "Mlada." Similarly we can only suppose that the figure in Ex. 59 suggested the idea of waves to *his* mind as definitely as Wagner's flickerings at the end of "Die Walküre" suggest leaping flames to almost everyone's. But in Korsakov's case the achievement falls far short of the intention. Even when we are told what it is supposed to be, we cannot with the best will in the world, see in it more than a rhythmical figure totally lacking in pictorial suggestiveness.

Rimsky-Korsakov's tone-painting is delightfully effective in a vague decorative way, but it lacks precision and real suggestive power. (The "bumble bee" music, part of which is so often played as a concert piece, is a different matter; the suggestion is purely aural and it is, after all, not very difficult for a composer to buzz effectively.) To say this, however, is not to imply that the composer *arbit-*

rarily associated themes like Ex. 59 with "waves" or what not. A visual object may suggest music without the music in return suggesting the same object. The definite is more likely to suggest the indefinite than vice versa. Take, for instance, Mussorgsky's "Intermezzo in modo classico" (not a piece of programme music), the chief theme of which, "rising and falling *à la Bach*," was—we know on the authority of the composer himself—spontaneously suggested to him by the sight of peasants plunging through soft snow on a bright winter's day. Given this clue, it is easy to see the connection. But it is noteworthy that even to the composer, though the peasants had suggested the theme, the theme suggested, not the peasants, but other music—Bach's. There is evidence that a great many of Rimsky-Korsakov's musical ideas were suggested in precisely the same way, but they are suggestive in turn only when they are definitely pantomimic.

For the rest, the most potent fuel that fed Rimsky-Korsakov's creative power was, of course, recollection of folk-songs. There are a number of actual folk-tunes in "Tsar Saltan": part of the dialogue of the elder sisters in the prologue, the lullaby in Act I,* the old man's tale, the nurses' clapping song, the theme of the youthful Tsar-

---

* This melody was introduced in memory of a nurse who had been accustomed to sing it to the composer's children and who had died the year before.

evich, the sailors' chorus in Act III, the flute theme of the singing squirrel, the old man's theme in the finale of the opera. But the influence of folk-song pervades the whole score. It is characteristic that the first bar of the Swan Princess's part in the love-duet with Guidon (the opening of a well-known folk-tune*) and the second bar (one of her own motives, invented by Rimsky-Korsakov himself) should so balance and complete each other that they sound like a single spontaneous musical thought:

One wonders again and again whether such actual reminiscences of fragments of folk-melody were intentional or unconscious, though such wonderings are as futile as Browning's speculation as to "who fished the murex up." What does matter is that the composer, knowingly or not, has made these scraps of tune his own. By fitting them into his pattern so perfectly, he has established his right to them. And in turn they provide that pattern with one of the most potent elements of its charm.

That, perhaps, is why there is no clairvoyance in the charm. The unreal world of "Saltan" is no true fairy world, no shadowing forth of an ideal world in which we can temporarily live ourselves. It is

---

* Used by Tchaikovsky in his "Oprichnik."

the everyday world—stylised, seen humorously, seen with unnatural sharpness of definition, fantastically decorated. Its delightfulness is due to *flavour*—and to flavour alone.

And that is the essential weakness of Rimsky-Korsakov's music as a whole. To hear it is a sensation—a delightful, a unique sensation—but never an experience.

XI.—NEW LIGHT ON OLD FRIENDS.

(A) The Programme of "Scheherazade."

When one considers how the musical world is (and always has been) infested with little Peterkins wanting to know "what it is all about," it seems all the more curious that so little is generally known of such a familiar work as Rimsky-Korsakov's "Scheherazade." Perhaps the curiosity of the little Peterkins was satisfied by the scenario fitted to the music for the Dyaghilev Ballet, though, except as regards the title, the scenario actually has no point of connection whatever with the music. Or it may be that the vague, non-committal "programme" (which is no programme at all) prefixed to the score and the innocently symmetrical build of the music, obviously not conditioned by any literary programme, have deceived them into accepting "Scheherazade" simply as absolute music with a fantastic, oriental flavour.

In doing so, they are not altogether wrong. And they would certainly have pleased the composer, for Rimsky-Korsakov wished his suite to be listened to as purely symphonic music. But he was anxious that "the listener should have the impression that the music is concerned with an oriental tale, describing a motley succession of fantastic happenings, and does not consist merely of four pieces played one after the other and based on the same thematic material,"* and to that end (and "because certain details of the musical construction suggest that all these stories are told by one and the same person") he gave the suite a title "connected in everyone's mind with the legendary splendour of the East" and added a prefatory note reminding the listener who Scheherazade was, and of the nature of her stories and the circumstances in which she told them.

On the other hand, although in the final edition of "Scheherazade" the individual movements are without titles, it is well known that they were originally called "The Sea and Sinbad's Ship," "The Tale of the Kalender Prince," "The Young Prince and the Young Princess" and "Festival in Bagdad: and the Shipwreck on the Rock with the Bronze Warrior." And these separate titles, suggesting the presence of a strongly programmatic element in the work, are reproduced in an edition widely used in this country and frequently appear in concert programmes. What are the real facts of the case? How far is "Scheherazade" "pure" music and how far programmatic? Fortunately

---
* "Memoirs," Chapter XX.

the composer himself, in his "Memoirs," took considerable pains to make this clear; but the "Memoirs" were written in 1906, eighteen years after the composition of "Scheherazade," and in the interval he appears either to have forgotten or to have deliberately suppressed a number of quasi-programmatic points of which he had made no secret in earlier years. Thus V. V. Yastrebtsev in his "Reminiscences of Rimsky-Korsakov," records two conversations (on March 18 and April 20, 1893) in which the composer, while affirming that his work was in no way a detailed musical reproduction of any of Scheherazade's stories, but only a series of recollections, or even a mere "general impression," of the tales, revealed the origin of several passages to which he gave no clue in his own "Memoirs."

So, from one source or another, we have a great deal of information as to what suggested the various details of the work, though the literary influence was practically limited to the suggestion of themes and had little or no influence on their connection or working-out. A character would suggest a theme; but the theme, instead of being treated as a sort of leitmotive of the character, is used like any abstract subject in a classical symphony, or may even be used as the motive of some other character in another part of the work. "For instance," says Rimsky-Korsakov in his "Memoirs," "the sharply defined fanfare theme from the 'Tale of the Kalender Prince' (second movement) also appears in the fourth movement in the description of the ship being dashed to pieces, although these episodes have nothing to do with each other." (He told Yastrebtsev that this theme "characterises the Bronze Warrior" when it appears in the fourth movement.) "The chief theme of the Kalender Prince (B minor, 3-4) and the theme of the Princess in the third movement (B flat, 6-8, clarinet) appear in somewhat different forms and in quicker *tempo* as secondary themes in the description of the festival in Bagdad, although nothing is said in the 'Thousand and One Nights' about their being there. The unison phrase at the beginning of the suite, depicting Scheherazade's cruel husband, also turns up in the 'Tale of the Kalender Prince,' where there can be no question of the Sultan Schariar." The only true leitmotive in the work is that of Scheherazade herself—the solo violin theme in the introductions to the first, second and fourth movements and in the middle of the third movement.

The constantly changing significance of the themes is exemplified at the very beginning of the first movement, where a slight modification of the "Schariar" theme is at once used in the "sea" music. According to Yastrebtsev, the *allegro non troppo* paints "the sea—with white-crested waves." (E major was a "dark blue" key to Rimsky-Korsakov, who was afflicted with an excessively keen sense of definite association between keys and colours). And the *tranquillo* chord passage which occurs three times in the course of the movement is a suggestion of Sinbad's smoothly sailing ship. Rimsky-Korsakov drew Yastrebtsev's attention to the "narrative character" of the second movement ("The Tale of the Kalender Prince"), "in the highest degree capricious and fantastic," adding that in the pages heralded by the fanfare "one might see a fight" and that the passages for two piccolos in the ensuing *vivace scherzando* were "a sort of musical sketch of Sinbad's bird, the roc." The composer was less definite about the third movement, "although, of course," he said, "the beginning sketches the Prince and the middle the Princess." And he added that the long-drawn crescendo of this middle part might be taken as depicting a sort of procession—"they carry the Princess in a palanquin."

Rimsky-Korsakov's original intention was to call his four movements simply "Prelude," "Ballade," "Adagio" (the *tempo* direction is actually *andantino quasi allegretto*), and "Finale," but on the advice of Lyadov and others he substituted the familiar titles "in order to give the hearer a hint as to the direction taken by my own imagination, while I left the filling in of all details to the mood and fancy of each individual listener." These vague finger-posts were removed from the final edition only because they had set people looking for a too definite programme. Rimsky-Korsakov's indecision—his attempt to eat his cake and have it, as it were—is amusing and rather characteristic of the man. Indeed, these little revelations throw as much light on the composer's mind in general as on "Scheherazade" itself. And, in addition, they provide a further valuable illustration of the way in which non-musical ideas frequently generate musical ones without leaving recognisable marks on them.

(B) THE PROGRAMME OF THE "PATHÉTIQUE" SYMPHONY.

"What song the Sirens sang" is still as much a matter of conjecture as it was in the days of Sir Thomas Browne, but the more modern puzzles of music are being cleared up one by one. Two or three years ago an ingenious investigator found that the "hidden theme" of Elgar's "Enigma" Variations is probably, if not certainly, "Auld Lang Syne"—a most appropriate motto for a work dedicated to the "friends pictured therein." And news recently came from Russia of the discovery of what is almost certainly the mysterious secret "programme" of Tchaïkovsky's "Pathétique" Symphony.

Tchaïkovsky intended the programme to remain for ever secret. "During the journey" (i.e., in December, 1892), "I got hold of the idea for a new symphony," he wrote in February, 1893, to his favourite nephew. "This time a programme-symphony, but with a programme that shall remain an enigma for everyone—let them puzzle their heads over it. The symphony will be called simply 'Programme Symphony' (No. 6). This programme is subjective through and through, and, while composing it in my mind, I often wept bitterly."

The Symphony was completed in August and performed on October 28—but simply as "Symphony in B minor," though a rumour seems to have got about in St. Petersburg that it had a secret programme. But Tchaïkovsky had given up the idea of frankly styling it "Programme Symphony." "Why 'programme symphony,' when I'm not going to give the programme?" he said. The morning after the concert, his brother Modest with whom he was staying found him still puzzling over the question of a title. Modest suggested that he should call it a "Tragic" Symphony, but the composer did not care for the idea.

"I left the room," says Modest in his biography of his brother, "before Peter had come to a decision. Suddenly the title 'Pathétique' occurred to me. I went back into the room—I remember it all as clearly as if it had happened yesterday—and told Peter of my idea. 'Splendid, Modi, bravo, *Pathétique!*' And in my presence he wrote down the title it has borne ever since." Yet, although the manuscript was actually sent to the publisher with that title, Tchaikovsky changed his mind the very next day and wrote asking that the Symphony should be published simply as "No. 6."

However, the name became known and perhaps helped to popularise the symphony. And ever since Modest's biography confirmed the rumour that it possessed a secret programme, ingenious minds have speculated concerning its nature. One ingenious critic even put forward a theory that it was political, a covert attack on the Tsar's government—in spite of the fact that Tchaïkovsky was well known to be a political reactionary and intensely loyal!

Now speculation is ended. Among Tchaïkovsky's papers in his old home at Klin (now a museum), with other notes and sketches relating to his last works, a sheet of music paper has recently come to light with the following notes scribbled in pencil:

"The ultimate essence of the plan of the symphony is LIFE. First part—all impulsive passion, confidence, thirst for activity. Must be short. (Finale DEATH—result of collapse.)

"Second part love; third disappointments; fourth ends dying away (also short)."

Admittedly this rough draft does not quite agree with the final version of the "Pathétique," but we can hardly doubt that it is the embryonic plan of it and that this is the solution of the enigma.

One point, admittedly, suggests a query. Tchaïkovsky's letter to his nephew is dated February 11-23, 1893, and these notes seem to belong to the year 1892 (judging from the other drafts and sketches among which they were found). Now in May, 1892, Tchaïkovsky began a Symphony in E flat, of which the first movement was afterwards converted into the Third Piano Concerto, Op. 75, while the *andante* and *finale* were also recast for piano and orchestra and published posthumously as Op. 79.

Does the newly discovered programme refer after all to this projected Symphony in E flat? I do not think so for a moment. For one thing, Op. 75 and Op. 79 do not appear to have the remotest connection with the programme; for another, the symphony as such was laid aside because it seemed to Tchaïkovsky "an empty pattern of sounds without genuine inspiration, written for the sake of writing," i.e., by no means a matter of life and death.

We may safely conclude either that the programme dates from the end of 1892 or that the basic idea of the "Pathétique" had been gestating in Tchaïkovsky's mind even before the journey to France in December, and that his statement to his nephew was not strictly accurate. Such an inaccuracy would be by no means an isolated case in Tchaikovsky's correspondence.

XII.—THE HISTORY OF "PRINCE IGOR."

Few famous operas can have a stranger history than "Prince Igor."

It is true the composition of "Siegfried" was spread over a period of twenty years, reckoning from the beginning of the poem of "The Young Siegfried" to the completion of the full score, and was interrupted for nearly a decade—an interval in which Wagner threw off such trifles as "Tristan" and "Die Meistersinger." But even "Siegfried" had a less eventful history than this Russian work begun in 1869, the very year that the actual composition of "Siegfried" was finished, and still far from complete when the composer died in 1887. (Compared with these elephantine feats of gestation, the rabbit-like fertility of Donizetti, with his steady average of rather more than two operas a year for thirty years, seems almost comic; and one feels heightened respect for a man like Rossini who could turn out such a masterpiece of its kind as "The Barber" in thirteen days.)

By 1869 Borodin had already tried his wings

twice in opera. In 1867 he had produced anonymously a *buffo* pastiche, "The Bogatïrs," and on Balakirev's advice he had, at about the same time, begun with a good deal of enthusiasm a setting of Mey's "The Tsar's Bride" (the subject used thirty years later by Rimsky-Korsakov), but had soon abandoned it. In January, 1869, his remarkable Symphony in E flat had its first performance and, encouraged by its success, he at once began the much better known Symphony in B minor. But he still hankered after the stage; he "would rather write an opera than a symphony," he said; and he worried Stassov to find him a suitable subject. On the evening of April 17-29,* he and Stassov again talked the matter over at the house of Lyudmila Shestakova, Glinka's sister, and that night the critic hit on a theme which he felt "met all the demands of Borodin's talent and artistic nature: broad epic motives, nationalism, variety of characters, passion, drama, the oriental." This was the twelfth century prose-poem, "The Story of Igor's Army," the Slavonic counterpart of the "Nibelungenlied" and the "Chanson de Roland." Early the next morning (Good Friday), Stassov set to work to sketch out a scenario based partly on the "Story" itself, partly on the "Ipatevsky Chronicle," a contemporary monkish account of the same historic events—which,

---

* Stassov himself says in his "Borodin" that it was the 19th, but his memory was at fault both as regards the date and in other trifling details.

incidentally, confirms the accuracy of the anonymous poet's narrative rather remarkably. Later in the day he was able to write to Borodin: "I am enclosing, Alexander Porfirievich, the whole scenarium...." And on Easter Sunday, the composer acknowledged his friend's assistance:

"I don't know how to thank you, dear Vladimir Vassilievich, for taking such a warm interest in my future opera.... Your plan is so full and detailed that everything is as clear as a bird's eye view; if any changes are necessary they will have to be in the way of shortenings.... I'm awfully keen on this idea. The only thing is: am I equal to it? I don't know. If you're afraid of wolves—don't go into the wood [a Russian proverb]. I will try."

This scenario of Stassov's disappeared for a long time and was first published as recently as 1922.* It consisted of ten large sheets of writing paper, divided in two, on one side being the details of the actual libretto, on the other the relevant excerpts from the original sources: the poem and the "Chronicle." It allowed for three acts divided into twelve scenes. It can only be summarised here, but this summary will suffice to show to what extent Borodin deviated from the original plan:

ACT I. (1) Igor's wife, Efrosinya Yaroslavna, alone in her apartments, sad and uneasy at the lack of news from her husband, worried by her brother's

---

* "Borodin." By E. M. Braudo. Petrograd, 1922.

behaviour, tormented by a dream of ill omen. (2) Her dissolute brother, Vladimir Yaroslavich (Prince Galitsky) bursts in and roughly tells her that Igor must be dead; *he* is now Prince of Seversk. (3) Yaroslavna's women inform her that merchants have arrived in Putivl with news of the army. The apartment fills with boyars and attendants, Galitsky's foreign followers—Germans, Venetians, Greeks and Moors—and finally the merchants. When Yaroslavna learns that the army is beaten and Igor and his son taken prisoner, she faints. But on her recovery the merchants tell the story (turn and turn about) in detail; how they came to be witnesses of the battle; how Igor attacked in spite of the omen of the eclipse and was at first victorious; of his heroism, his wound and his capture. Galitsky's followers proceed to sing the praises of Igor's father, who had always beaten the Polovtsi, and to jeer at Igor; Galitsky proclaims himself Prince of Seversk and is hailed first by the foreigners, then by the Russian boyars. Only the women weep for Igor. (4) Yaroslavna is left alone in despair. Suddenly she thinks of Ovlur, a Polovtsian captive, who nevertheless has Russian blood in his veins and is personally devoted to Igor and herself. She sends for him and, imploring his help, unfolds her plan. As a Polovtsian he will be welcomed back in the enemy camp and will soon be able to get access to Igor and help him to escape. Ovlur agrees willingly : " It is his dream to do some-

The History of "Prince Igor." 151

thing great and good for Russia, Igor and Yaroslavna."

ACT II. (5) The luxurious tent of the Polovtsian khan, Konchak. Love-scene between his daughter Konchakovna and Igor's son, Vladimir Igorevich, who tells her he is willing to give up everything for her sake, even to become a Polovtsian if his father remains adamant in forbidding their marriage. Startled by the sound of hunting-horns, the lovers slip away. (6) Igor, with a suite of Russians and Polovtsians, returns from a hawking expedition—gloomy and self-reproachful. (7) Konchak appears, reproves Igor for his moodiness (for his captivity is far from unpleasant) and reminds him that they are old friends and had been comrades in war only a few years before. Let him marry Vladimir to Konchakovna, take a Polovtsian wife himself, and settle down as a Polovtsian chieftain. Igor thanks him and assures him of his personal affection, but rejects the offer; he is devoted to Russia and Yaroslavna. Konchak becomes angry. (8) But the stage fills with people, including the young lovers, and there are dances. The girls jeer at the Russians. Another Polovtsian force enters, fresh from the sack of Pereyaslavl, and the rejoicing of the Polovtsi becomes wilder than ever. (9) Igor, alone with his son and the other prisoners, prays to God to send him death if he can be of no more use to his native land. At this point Ovlur appears, tells him of the happenings in Putivl and suggests that he should break his word and fly. Igor refuses to do anything so shameful, but Ovlur reminds him of the numerous precedents; the other Russians add their persuasion; and Igor finally agrees. (10) Edge of the Polovtsian camp at night; tents on one side, forest on the other, river in background. Intoxication of the guards. Igor tries to persuade his son to escape too, but Konchakovna holds him back. Ovlur's whistle is heard. Igor escapes into the forest. The Polovtsi appear too late to catch him.

Act III. (11) Early morning on the walls of Putivl. Yaroslavna's lament, taken direct from the old poem.* Sound of horses. Yaroslavna recognises her husband. After a joyful reunion, they quickly reckon up the still loyal boyars in Putivl and decide on measures first against Galitsky, then against the foreign enemy. (12) Two years later. Festival in Putivl: the wedding of Konchakovna and Vladimir Igorevich. From the songs and rejoicing it appears that Igor has imprisoned Vladimir Galitsky and got rid of his treacherous subjects. Final chorus in praise of the Russian princes and of Russian arms.

It will be noticed that, among other important differences from the final version, the comic *gudok*-players, Eroshka and Skula, make no appearance in

---

* An English version of the lament is given in Maurice Baring's "Outline of Russian Literature" (Home University Library).

Stassov's draft. Indeed, the First Act as we know it has only two or three points in common with the original plan. The merchants have disappeared and the act ends with a tocsin scene. Ovlur also is cut out, so that his appearance in the Polovtsian camp in the next act remains unexplained and he appears there to be only a common traitor. Nor are the relations between Igor and Konchak very clear in the final version, though the point is of minor importance. Still, the Second and Third Acts together correspond fairly closely to Stassov's Act II, and the Fourth is simply a modification (at the end) of Stassov's Scene 11. The epilogue (Scene 12) has disappeared altogether and the opera has gained in compensation a prologue and an entirely new scene at the beginning of Act I.

At first, however, Borodin accepted Stassov's scenario just as it stood, writing his own libretto a bit at a time, more or less simultaneously with the music mated with it. All through the summer he busied himself with the gathering of non-musical material, steeping himself in the atmosphere of the old Slavonic legends, reading other old poems and songs, commentaries on "The Song of Igor's Army," prose and verse versions of it in modern Russian and so on. Through a friend, he made the acquaintance of the Hungarian traveller, Hunfalvy, who gave him scraps of native melody he had noted down in Central Asia, and, curiously enough, among the descendants of the ancient Polovtsi now settled in certain parts of Hungary.*

The actual composition of the music was not begun till September. "Notwithstanding the host of things I have on hand" (i.e., professional duties), he writes to his wife on the 21st (October 3), "I've managed to do the first number of Act I of 'Igor,' though not quite all. Have not shown it to anyone yet." This was "Yaroslavna's dream," her arioso at the beginning of Act I, Scene 2. Twelve days later he informs her that "Yaroslavna's dream has turned out delightfully." But instead of working steadily through the opera, Borodin first tackled the points that specially took his fancy. Konchakovna's cavatina was one of the next numbers, and it appears from another letter to his wife (March 4-16, 1870) that he had "been trying to make some numbers from the materials I had already prepared." That is, Stassov says, materials from the

* In my "Studies in Russian Music" (page 136), speaking of the melody of the opening chorus of Act II, I pointed out that "it is clearly either genuine raw material or material in only the first stage of manufacture. Either Borodin got most of his 'Polovtsian' cliches from this tune or he took this opportunity of making a synthesis of nearly all the features he had observed to be characteristic of the folk-music he wished to imitate; and of the two, the former seems decidedly the more reasonable supposition." S. A. Dyanin, the son of Borodin's friend and executor, Alexander Dyanin, who is preparing the definitive Russian life of the composer, writes me: "You are quite right: I had the good fortune to discover (in 1928) the song in question—or, rather, the folk-theme which is the basis of all the principal choruses in the opera."

The History of "Prince Igor." 155

abandoned "Tsar's Bride"; it seems probable that the chorus of khans in Act III originated as a chorus of *oprichniks* in the earlier opera. But in this very same letter Borodin announces that he has abandoned "Igor" also and is dedicating a song to Stassov "to soften the blow." "I can't be bothered with the opera," he goes on. It would cost an enormous amount of time and trouble; production is uncertain and, even if it were assured, there would be further bother with the theatre authorities and the artists:

"Besides: the subject, however suitable for music, would hardly go down with the public. There is scarcely any drama or scenic movement. Moreover, the making of a libretto satisfactory from both musical and scenic points of view is no joke. I haven't enough of either experience, skill or time for it. . . . Anyhow, opera (not dramatic in the strict sense) seems to me an unnatural thing. This was sharply brought home to me after I'd heard 'Le Prophète' on the Maryinsky stage. Besides, I am by nature a lyricist and a symphonist; I am attracted to the symphonic forms."

And he reassured Stassov that the music he had composed for "Igor" would not be wasted. "It will all go into my Second Symphony."

Accordingly "Igor" was given up definitely as "The Tsar's Bride" had been a year or two before. Professional duties pressed; Borodin had little time for music; and it was late in 1871 before even the first movement of the Second Symphony was finished. Then early in 1872 came the commission for the collaborative "Mlada."* As we have seen, the Fourth Act of this work fell to Borodin's share, and he turned to account for it some of the music composed for "Igor," adding a great deal of fresh material. But "Mlada" in turn fell through and Borodin returned to his Second Symphony.

Then in the autumn or winter of 1874, partly owing to the persuasion of a young friend and ex-pupil at the Army Medical Academy, V. A. Shonorov, Borodin again began to interest himself in "Igor." Loath to waste his "Mlada" music, he transferred nearly the whole of it in a more or less expanded form to "Igor" and at the same time subjected Stassov's plan to a vigorous reconstruction—of which the other approved, however. The most important changes consisted of the amputation of the Epilogue (the wedding feast), and the addition of a prologue (Igor's departure for war) and what is now the first scene of Act I. It is probable that some of the thematic material of the Epilogue had already been used as the basis of the slow movement and finale of the Second Symphony (whence, no doubt, Stassov's rather unconvincing story that the *andante* is intended to depict an old Slavonic bard, and the finale a feast of warrior-heroes). And we know definitely that the opening chorus of the

---

* See Chapter VIII.

Prologue was intended in the first instance for the Epilogue. But most of the Prologue music was derived from "Mlada," largely that associated with the priests and worship of Radegast. The eclipse described by the merchants in Stassov's Scene 3 was now actually shown in the Prologue, apparently as an excuse for using up the effective "ghost" music written for "Mlada." In addition to the Prologue music, Borodin proposed to turn a duet between Yaromir and Voyslava into the trio just before Igor's escape; though as we shall see, he never did so. A scene between Yaromir and the chief priest provided material for some of Igor's self-communings. At the same time the two clowns, Eroshka and Skula, were introduced in the Prologue, in the new first scene of Act I (the courtyard of Galitsky's house) and in the final scene, their parts gradually developing to such an extent that Borodin used to say jokingly that the opera ought to be called not "Prince Igor" but "The Gudok-Players." And two magnificent new numbers were composed: Yaroslavna's lament (revised the following year) and the famous Polovtsian march—the latter, according to Mme. Borodina, "inspired by the reading of a traveller's description of executions among the Japanese." Writing to Lyubov Karmalina in April, 1875, Borodin, after giving her a semi-humorous account of his being unable to compose except "when too unwell to do anything *sensible*," goes on to inform her:

"I've written the big march of the Polovtsi, Yaroslavna's aria, Yaroslavna's lament for the last act, a little female chorus in the Polovtsian camp, and something for the dances (oriental—as the Polovtsi were an oriental people). I've already accumulated a lot of materials and even completed numbers (e.g., choruses, Konchakovna's aria, etc.). But when shall I manage to finish all this? I'm blessed if I know."

The famous choral dances were finished in Moscow later in the summer, together with Konchak's aria (originally written in B major) and the opening chorus of Act I—all of which delighted Stassov and the other members of the "handful." It really looked as if the opera were going to be completed. But work soon began to slow down, in spite of the fact that the Second Symphony was finished, and so out of the way, by 1876. "You ask about 'Igor?'" he writes to Mme. Karmalina (June, 1876):

"When I talk about it, it seems quite funny even to myself. I am reminded of Finn in 'Ruslan.' Just as he, dreaming of his love for Naina, doesn't notice that time is flying, constantly flying . . . so I try to realise my ardent dream—to write an epic Russian opera. Time hurries away post-haste; days, weeks, months, winters pass under conditions that make it impossible for me to think of seriously occupying myself with music. It's not that I can't snatch a couple of leisure hours a day; no, but I have no mental leisure, no chance of getting out of

The History of "Prince Igor." 159

the daily round of cares and of thoughts that have nothing in common with art . . . of getting oneself re-tuned into a musical frame of mind, without which creative work on a large scale, as with an opera, is unthinkable. My only chance to get into that mood is during part of the summer. In the winter I can write music only when I'm just too unwell to lecture or go to the laboratory, but well enough to do something. . . . Thus, for instance, last Christmas I had 'flu and couldn't go to the laboratory, so I stayed at home and wrote the chorus of glorification for the last act of 'Igor.'"*

In September, 1876, held up on a journey by a river in flood, he improvised Yaroslavna's recitative in the last act (p. 318 of the vocal score), under the gloomy impression produced by the grey, scurrying, leaping water. And in much the same haphazard way other numbers (together, it is true, with the A major String Quartet) followed during the next year or so. The well-known recitative and cavatina, "Slowly the daylight fades," was composed in 1877 "under the impression of a somewhat romantic circumstance," his wife tells us. "A young girl fell passionately in love with Alexander, and he had considerable difficulty in turning her into a 'daughter!'" In August of the following year came the rest of the scene in Galitsky's courtyard,

---

* Afterwards transferred to the Prologue, part of it *before* the eclipse scene, etc., part of it after. It was also transposed from G to C.

the song of the *gudok*-players (p. 60 of the vocal score) and the choral ensembles. In August, 1879, again on his summer holiday in the country, Borodin writes to Stassov:

"I've made a real character of Vladimir Galitsky, who had so far had only two or three words of recitative: I've given him a couple of recitatives and a very cynical song, characterising his attitude to things in general and to Yaroslavna in particular. This is an interpolation in the choral scene of the first tableau of Act I. For the second tableau I've written a duet for Vladimir Galitsky and Yaroslavna; a female chorus [the first one (p. 86); the second in 5-4 time was added the year after] and a little scene with Yaroslavna, all throwing the character of Vladimir Galitsky into higher relief. . . . I'm now working at the finale of Act I. In this I've made a deviation from the original plan of the libretto, for which you will perhaps reproach me. Instead of letting the merchants themselves communicate the news about Igor and the disaster at the Kayala, this is done by the boyars and attendants who have already heard the terrible news from the merchants. They come to prepare the Princess . . . she learns the truth, faints, comes round and asks who has brought the news; then orders the merchants to be brought to her to give details. This is done so as to avoid the narration of the merchants . . . [The music already composed for their narration was afterwards used for the trio of the Third

The History of "Prince Igor." 161

Symphony.] If the narration were made full, poetic and picturesque as in the original, it would be intolerably long and boring—and, after all, nobody will hear the words; the grandiose music demanded by the circumstances couldn't be given to a couple of second-rate singers (and the first-raters would be needed for the other rôles) and it would all be much more wishy-washy than if the chorus did it. The only effective point in the libretto was that the merchants narrate 'turn and turn about.' But this is a purely superficial effect."

Later these inessential merchants disappeared altogether.

Rimsky-Korsakov tells us in his memoirs of his desperate attempts at this period to get Borodin at least to orchestrate some of the numbers for concert performance:

"The host of professorial duties and his Medical Courses for Women constantly hindered him. . . . I used to go again and again to ask how much he had done. It was never more than a page or two of the score! You asked him: 'Alexander Porfirievich, have you been writing anything?' and he would say, 'Of course, I have.' But it would turn out that he had been writing nothing but a lot of letters."

Korsakov had already announced three numbers for performance at his Free School concerts early in 1879 and was rehearsing the chorus. But although Konchak's aria was orchestrated, the scoring of the Polovtsian dances and the final chorus of the opera was far from complete. Finally, in despair, Korsakov induced the composer to accept his help:

"So he came to me in the evenings with his unfinished score of the dances, and the three of us—he, Lyadov and I—divided it up and set to work. For greater speed, we wrote with pencils instead of ink, sitting far into the night. When the pages of score were finished, Borodin covered them with liquid gelatine so that the pencillings should not get rubbed out, and the sheets were hung up on lines to dry in my study, like so much washing."

Much the same happened the next year, though this time Borodin did his own orchestration (of Yaroslavna's lament, Vladimir Galitsky's song, and the scene of Yaroslavna with the girls), and Rimsky-Korsakov did not exaggerate when he claimed that "but for the Free School concerts the fate of 'Prince Igor' would have been very different."

Yet the fate of "Igor" was unhappy enough as it was. Borodin had still half-a-dozen years to live but, apart from the eternal routine of duty and the domestic disturbances caused by his wife's chronic ill-health, he was diverted from his opera by the composition of "In Central Asia" (1880) and the Second String Quartet (1881-2). To make things worse, an attack of cholera in the middle of the 'eighties seriously affected his creative power. The final version of Igor's big aria, possibly sketched earlier, was written in the autumn of 1881 or soon after, but there is very little evidence in the Borodin documents so far published that he worked at all at his opera for four or five years. A few weeks before his death he devised one or two things—for instance, the overture and the chorus of Russian prisoners in Act II—which he played over to his friends but never bothered to write down; and in February, 1887, just before the sudden end, he composed the chorus of the Polovtsian patrol, which follows the chorus of prisoners, and the recitative dialogue of Igor and Konchak (pp. 192-6) preceding the dances that end Act II. But when Rimsky-Korsakov and Glazunov undertook to complete and orchestrate "Prince Igor" after their friend's death, they were able to find only about eight numbers of the whole opera finished and scored; the rest consisted partly of complete sections in piano score, partly of very rough sketches. As for the Second and Third Acts Rimsky-Korsakov tells us, they could find:

"No libretto or even scenario,* but only single

---

* S. A. Dyanin has recently discovered the following rough scenario for Act III, scribbled in the back of the draught of a letter to S. I. Taneev (January, 1876):

3 act, I Scene. Igor's Tent.

(1) Duet of Vladimir and Konchakovna (*Konchakovna* alone better?)

(2) Igor comes in with his people. Konchakovna hides herself *behind the tapestry.* (Music of the shades [i.e., from "Mlada"] and *ninths*). Grey-headed, trustworthy groom and others urge the Prince to flee.—Ovlur,—Prince agrees—

verses and musical sketches, or numbers completed but quite disconnected. I was well acquainted with the content of both acts from my talks with Borodin, although he altered a great deal in his plans, taking things out and putting others in."

The two musical executors lost no time in setting to work,* the elder collaborator scoring the Prologue, Acts I, II and IV, and the famous march which opens Act III, the younger completing and orchestrating the overture and the rest of the Third Act. They finished their labour by the summer of 1888; Belaiev published it; and the first performance was given at the Maryinsky Theatre, Petersburg, on October 23-November 4, 1890.

How much of "Prince Igor" was actually composed by Rimsky-Korsakov and Glazunov to fill up Borodin's lacunæ, then? Fortunately Glazunov, at Stassov's request, wrote in 1891 an exact

---

2 Scene (3rd act).

(3) *Ovlur goes to the guards, dance; guards oversleep.*

(4) **Flight**, quartet, scena (from the "Mlada" duet).

(5) **Alarm.** They seize Vladimir, want to kill him, etc. (Gzak, Konchakovna).

(6) **Appearance of Konchak**, they tell him about Igor ("There's a fine fellow," "there's a wife for you"), (grumbling of Gzak), prepare to march.

All saddle.
        Flood Music, [i.e., from "Mlada"].

* It can hardly be a mere coincidence that the idea of "Scheherazade" occurred to Rimsky-Korsakov while he was scoring the oriental second act of "Igor."

account* of their stewardship, an account which incidentally demolishes the legend of his own feat of "writing out the overture entirely from memory of the composer's performance on the piano," and moreover exposes Rimsky-Korsakov once again to the familiar charge of having exceeded his duty as a musical executor:

"The overture was composed by me roughly according to Borodin's plan. I took the themes from the corresponding numbers of the opera and was fortunate enough to find the canonic ending of the second subject among the composer's sketches. I slightly altered the fanfares for the overture. (The fanfares after the words, 'Sound, trumpets!' [p. 250 of the vocal score] belong entirely to Borodin. The idea of the fanfares is preserved in the overture, but I changed their sequence.) The bass progression in the middle I found noted down on a scrap of paper, and the combination of the two themes (Igor's aria and a phrase from the trio) was also discovered among the composer's papers. A few bars at the very end were composed by me. *Prologue and Act I.* The Prologue remains without change or addition. So does the first scene of the First Act. In the second scene Rimsky-Korsakov composed a little transitional recitative after Vladimir Galitsky's exit until the entry of the boyars ('My whole body trembles') [p. 105]. The tocsin

---

* Published in the "Russian Musical Gazette" in 1896, but strangely overlooked by later writers.

was found sketched out, and Rimsky-Korsakov made some additions to it, e.g., the wailing of the women behind the scenes. *Act II.* I composed the very beginning of the Second Act (a few chords) as the composer had begun straight away with the entry of the voice (the Polovtsian girl's song). Rimsky-Korsakov touched up the dance a little by adding in one or two places a quintuple chromatic rising phrase against the 6-8 rhythm. In Konchakovna's cavatina Rimsky-Korsakov added the chorus, which Borodin had not employed. The recitative after Konchakovna's cavatina was composed by Rimsky-Korsakov. The Russian chorus [the chorus of prisoners] was written down by me from memory—I had heard Borodin play it—but I do not vouch for its complete accuracy; the words of this chorus were written by Rimsky-Korsakov. Of the orchestral passage at the beginning and end of the chorus, the first two bars are by Rimsky-Korsakov, the last two by me. We found Ovlur's recitative; but it was very difficult to work it in. The rest, right to the end, is as the composer left it. *Act III.* The march was entirely written by the composer, but orchestrated by Rimsky-Korsakov. I distinctly remembered the first two bars of Konchak's next song; the six following bars are my own continuation. At the words, 'After the battle at the Kayala' [top of p. 244], there are two more bars which we found on a scrap of paper. I remembered the choral cry: 'Hail to Gzak and Konchak,' from the composer's playing it; but he had given it to Konchak himself, not to the chorus. The rest, such as the connecting middle part of the song, was composed by me on the composer's themes (partly on the theme of the 'chorus of khans'). The ensuing recitative, 'Sound, trumpets!' and the fanfares are entirely by the composer; I copied them from his manuscript. I composed the whole of the music from the words, 'Now let us go and divide the spoil' [bottom of p. 250] to the end of the number, imitating Borodin's style as closely as possible. The chorus of the khans, the ensemble of the Russians and the scene of the arrival of the baggage-train with booty, but for some cuts, are just as Borodin wrote them. The chorus and dance of the guards were composed by me; on Rimsky-Korsakov's suggestion I introduced a phrase from the Polovtsian dances of the previous Act, treated as a two-part canon (the idea of the canon was also Rimsky-Korsakov's). The theme of the dance was found among the manuscripts, though without any indication where it was to be used; but in all probability it was intended for this passage. Ovlur's recitative was composed by me on the 'Ovlur theme.' The trio was written in this way: the 'Mlada' duet was inserted whole, as Borodin had always intended, though it was necessary to re-arrange the parts; Igor's cry was taken from his aria; and we discovered the intermediate music (as in the overture)—which was obviously intended for

'Igor's flight,' being a development of the chief theme of the trio. Part of the words of the trio had been written under the music by Borodin himself; I had to write the rest. I composed the finale up to the chorus of khans, 'Konchak, let us hold a council' [p. 297]; all the rest is the composer's, only with my ornamentation added to give the music a nuptial, festive character. I composed the preceding part on themes from the rest of the opera (viz., from Konchak's aria, the chorus of khans, the trio, the scene of the baggage-train, etc.). There was no scenario for the Third Act and Rimsky-Korsakov had to write one,* preserving many of the composer's own words and his intentions; where words were missing Rimsky-Korsakov and I wrote them. *Act IV.* This is entirely Borodin's."

In view of this statement, and considering what we know of Rimsky-Korsakov's treatment of "Boris," "Khovanshchina" and "The Stone Guest," it would be interesting to know whether he also made melodic and harmonic "improvements" in "Igor." It is highly improbable that he refrained from doing so.

---

* It is interesting to compare the result with Borodin's own long-lost scenario (see page 163).

XIII.—BORODIN'S SONGS.

I think it was Sir Henry Hadow who once wrote that "few composers have challenged immortality with such a handful of masterpieces as Borodin." Hadow was thinking of Borodin's output in general, but his remark applies with peculiar force to Borodin's songs—a mere dozen in number yet nearly all of such quality that Findeisen, one of the soundest of Russian critics, felt obliged to devote nearly as much space to Borodin in his study of "The Russian Art-Song and its Development" as he did to Mussorgsky. Yet how often does one hear them? Russian musicians have long acknowledged the majority of them to be some of the finest flowers of their song-literature. And bating the objection on principle to all translated texts, the English singer has no excuse for neglecting them, for all but three are available with English words, and the three exceptions are provided with French versions.*

---

* Only eight of the songs were published during the composer's lifetime. Four of them, "The Song of the Dark Forest," "Aus meinen Tränen," "The Sea Princess," and "The Wond'rous Garden," are published by Bessel with English words by Edward

We first hear of Borodin writing songs (which he seems to have been ashamed to show anyone) in the 'fifties while still a student at the Medical Academy, and of his being publicly reprimanded by Prof. Zinin for wasting his time on such frivolous pursuits. One of these songs, a setting of Heine's "Schönes Fischermädchen," written for an amateur "contralto" who is said to have had a three-octave compass (from C to C!), is said by Khubov* to 'bear an obviously imitative, sentimental-dilettantish character.' But none of these early efforts were ever published. The first of Borodin's serious essays in song-writing, "The Sleeping Princess," dates from 1867, the year of the completion of the First Symphony. The following year came four real masterpieces—"An Old Song" ("Song of the Dark Forest"), "The False Note," "The Sea Princess," and a setting of Heine's "Vergiftet sind meine Lieder."

All these songs, except the last, are settings of Borodin's own words. Like Mussorgsky, he had a peculiar gift, not for writing independently satisfac-

---

Agate. The others came out from Jurgenson (now the Russian State Publishing Company); one of them, "The Sea," has been published by Chester with an English version by Rosa Newmarch, but the other three are obtainable only with French translations: "The Sleeping Princess," "The False Note" ("Dissonance") and "Vergiftet sind meine Lieder" (disguised as "Mon chant est amer et sauvage"). The four songs posthumously published by Belaiev are available with translations by Edward Agate.

* Georgy Khubov: "A. P. Borodin." Moscow, 1933.

tory poetry, but for finding exactly the right words for his own music. Such single-minded creation of poem and music has scarcely any parallel in the rest of the world's serious song-literature. Even in Wagner's case, poem and music were evidently the results of separate acts of creation. The libretto may have been conceived here and there more or less simultaneously with the music to be associated with it; but the very magnitude of an opera makes impossible that complete unity, or rather absolute artistic identity, of words and music which one is conscious of in Borodin's "False Note" and "Song of the Dark Forest," or in Mussorgsky's "Ragamuffin" and his "Nursery" songs. It is true Tchaïkovsky once set a poem of his own ("The Dread Minute," Op. 23, No. 6). But then he was no poet, whereas (according to Findeisen—for a non-Russian must tread warily on this part of the ground) from a literary point of view "the texts of Borodin and Mussorgsky are absolutely original and poetic."

"The desire of Borodin and his comrades to write songs was much assisted," says Stassov, "by the circumstance that their circle included the talented singer, Alexandra Molas" (*née* Purgold, whose sister afterwards married Rimsky-Korsakov). "All the compositions of the 'comrades' which could be managed by her female voice, were performed by her at their gatherings . . . and performed with such talent, deep truthfulness, passion and fineness of shading as inevitably acted on such impressionable and gifted people as the 'comrades' as a warm stimulus to fresh composition. . . . Borodin was often so carried away by Alexandra Purgold's wonderful performance that he openly told her that some of his songs had been composed 'by the two of them together.' He repeated this most often in connection with the seething passion of 'Vergiftet sind meine Lieder.'"

In 1869 Borodin began "Prince Igor" and his Second Symphony. Song-writing was neglected: but in March, 1870, as we have seen, he temporarily changed his mind about "Igor" and decided to abandon it. And in a letter in which he tells his wife this, he speaks also of "my new 'sea' ballad" ("The Sea."). "This production is valued extremely highly by the 'severe critics.' Many, including Balakirev, consider it better than 'The Princess' [i.e., "The Sleeping Princess"]—and that's a great deal. The thing really has turned out very well: plenty of passionate fire, brilliance, melodiousness, and everything in it very '*truly said*' musically. But I confess I was rather fearful about the thing: everyone thought it would turn out clumsily, awkwardly, and so on . . ." And then, after describing how all the circle are enraptured by it, he adds: "I've dedicated this thing to Bach [his nickname for Stassov]—first, because he has kept on worrying and pestering me to write it down [instead of playing it over and then forgetting it, as Borodin sometimes did]; secondly, so as to soften the blow of my definite refusal to go on with 'Igor.'"

The song in its first form had different words, though both sets were written by the composer. The published version speaks only of the shipwreck of "a mariner youthful and dauntless" who

> "steers straight for home, with rich booty untold:
> His ship with sweet spices and bright silks is laden:
> Jewels that sparkle, and caskets of gold;
> And one belov'd maiden."

But Stassov tells us that originally the music "depicted a young exile, obliged to leave his fatherland for political reasons, returning home—and tragically wrecked ... in sight of the very shores of his native land." Borodin was politically a Liberal; a letter of Mussorgsky's hints that even "the sleeping princess" awaiting the deliverer who will wake her to life, is a symbol of Russia; but it was probably as much as his official position was worth to publish a song expressing sympathy with political exiles.

After "The Sea" Borodin wrote no more songs for a whole decade. He returned to "Igor," completed his Second Symphony, and wrote his first String Quartet. Then about 1880 came another

Heine setting, "Aus meinen Tränen," heralding another little dribble of songs during the last few years of the composer's life. In 1881, suggested by Mussorgsky's death, came "For the shores of thy far native land," a setting of Pushkin. (Agate's translation is called "It was thy choice, far journey taking.") The connection with Mussorgsky is probably to be found in the hint at his well-known motto, "Toward new shores!"—but musically the song shows no trace of any such striving. It is the most conventional of all Borodin's songs and bears more eloquent testimony to his love of Schumann than to his admiration of the musical ideals of his dead comrade. "It contains little deep and sincere feeling," says Stassov, "as the composer himself fully admitted; in accordance with his own wish and the opinion of his intimate friends, he refused to the end of his life to allow it to be printed." And generally speaking this second batch of half-a-dozen songs is altogether inferior to the first. The "Arabian Melody" (again to Borodin's own words, modelled on the texts of genuine Arabian songs) is a charming little essay in the pseudo-oriental, but no more. But two other songs break new ground —new, that is, for Borodin: "Pride," to words by Alexey Tolstoy, a satirical sketch, very slight musically, but strikingly effective—pen-and-ink caricature music; and "Rich and Poor" (1884), a setting of a poem by Nekrassov, full of typically Russian "pity," in which Borodin comes nearer than anywhere else in his songs to the music of the people. The last of all Borodin's songs, "Septains" ("The Wondrous Garden"), is merely a graceful tribute commemorating his visit to the Castle of Argenteau, near Liége, as the guest of the Comtesse de Mercy Argenteau, the well-known Belgian patroness of Russian music, and, incidentally, the last mistress of Napoleon III.* The original words were French —by a Belgian poet, "C. G."—though the published French text is a retranslation from the Russian.

Thus, few as these songs are in number, they are so diverse in style that they cover a wide range of expression, from the concentrated epigrammatic quality of "The False Note" to the picturesque narrative style of "The Sea," from the pure lyricism of "Aus meinen Tränen" to the epic manner of "The Song of the Dark Forest." Of the two long narrative songs, "The Sea" and "The Sleeping Princess," both styled *skazka* (legend, *ballade*), "The Sea" is first and foremost a piece of tone-painting for the pianoforte. But "The Sleeping Princess" has a charming vocal line, and the whole song is enveloped in an atmosphere of drowsy enchantment. The persistent syncopated seconds of the accompaniment:

---

* An English translation of her reminiscences appeared in 1926 with the title "The Last Love of an Emperor" (Heinemann).

61

were very daring sixty years ago and particularly infuriated Tchaïkovsky's friend, the academic critic. Laroche. "It is difficult to explain to the non-musical reader what an orgy of dissonance rages in this song," he wrote, "while the musical reader who has not seen the song will hardly believe that seconds, treated as consonances, continue without a break for several pages."

Both "The False Note" and "Vergiftet sind meine Lieder" are flawess little gems. Indeed "Falshivaya Nota"—just seventeen bars long—is perhaps the most perfect epigram in the whole range of vocal literature.* The "false note in her voice and in her heart" is symbolised by the F which persists throughout, and the point is under-

---

* It is hardly credible that one of Borodin's friends offered him four additional stanzas, which he was naturally obliged to reject.

lined by the whole-tone passage in the left hand. But there is a curious misprint in the Jurgenson edition. In the very bar which mentions the "false note," the engraver has contrived a couple of wrong notes on his own account—D flat, E natural (instead of F, G natural) in the right-hand pianoforte part.

Of the two Heine songs, "Vergiftet sind meine Lieder" is much the better. Hardly longer than "The False Note," it has the same quality of direct and concentrated expression. "Aus meinen Tränen" is charming but (even putting Schumann's setting out of one's mind) adequate rather than inevitable. But "Vergiftet sind meine Lieder" translates the words (of the Russian version, and almost equally those of the original poem) into music with such perfection that one could easily imagine both words and music, in this case, too, to be the fruit of one mind and a single creative impulse.

Nothing could be in sharper contrast with the exquisite civilisation of these songs than the primitive barbarism of "The Song of the Dark Forest," the only example in Borodin's songs of his heroic manner, the manner of "Igor" and the B minor Symphony. Yet it owes most of its value to precisely the same qualities as "The False Note" and "Vergiftet sind meine Lieder": directness and economy of expression, the vocal line following the poetic rhythm naturally and with complete freedom from conventional rhythmic patterns, yet always shaped to a satisfactory musical outline. "The Dark

Forest," very irregularly barred, has a melodic line which, on the one hand, seems to have come into being simultaneously with the words and, on the other, is as self-sufficient as an instrumental melody:

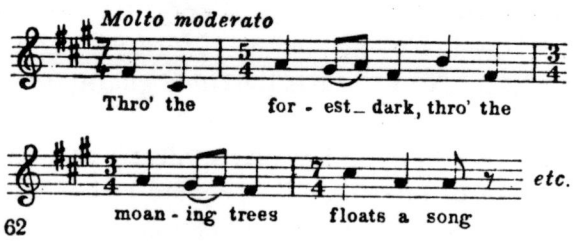

But all Borodin's songs are definitely lyrical (though "The Dark Forest" is less a lyric than a fragment from an unwritten epic). With all their "truth," they have little in common with Mussorgsky's songs. They represent, in fact, the golden mean between Mussorgsky's "truth" and Tchaïkovsky's rather shallow lyrical charm.

XIV.—BALAKIREV'S SYMPHONIES.

Fate has not behaved kindly with Balakirev. It is true he has his place, and a place of honour in the history of Russian music as the man who took the torch from Glinka and handed it to Borodin, Mussorgsky and Korsakov. But to lie embalmed for ever in the pages of history is, for the creative artist, a poor substitute for immortality. Kings and soldiers, most statesmen, and all actors, singers and players have to be content with it; but the poet, the painter and the composer hope for a real life after death. Not to have won it is for them to have failed. And Balakirev seems to have failed. One wonders why, for though there are various reasons why he did not achieve much more than he did—a "much more" that was clearly within his powers and which would have put him head and shoulders above all other nineteenth century Russians—they do not account for the neglect of his actual achievement. It is true his music is not all in limbo, but the only two of his compositions that are at all well-known, "Tamara" and "Islamey," represent only one side of his genius. Judging him solely by these two "oriental" works, no one would take him for the all-round master he is. The "Overture on Three Russian Themes," which the B.B.C. gives us opportunities of hearing from time to time, is an early work, charming and characteristic, but about as representative of the Balakirev of the two symphonies as "Prometheus" is of the Beethoven of the "Eroica" and the Seventh.

If you turn to "Grove" for information about Balakirev's symphonies you will, for once, catch him nodding. "Balakirev," he tells you, "wrote but one symphony in the strict sense of the word." (Indeed, not only the Second Symphony but a piano concerto, a piano sonata, and quite a number of other trifles slipped past his contributor in that nap.) Balakirev's First Symphony, in C major, was finished in 1898 and, curiously enough, had its first English performance almost at once. The composer was then sixty-one, an oldish man to be writing his first symphony. But—and this explains a good deal—quite a lot of it had been written thirty-two years before! Rimsky-Korsakov tells us that about a third of the first movement was already in score in 1866, and that the composer had made sketches for the second and fourth movements. So the work, if it were nothing more, would be a pretty curiosity, a symphony begun by a young man and ended by an ageing one. It took Balakirev fifteen years or so to compose "Tamara," but he was living with it in his mind all the time, "brooding" over it (to use his own phrase) and letting it slowly mature as a whole, only hesitating to put the definitive form on paper. But the symphony seems to have been a case of a rather different kind, to have been abandoned altogether and then taken up afresh after that astonishing interval. It is as if Beethoven had laid down the pen in the middle of the C major Symphony, almost given up composing, and then one fine day taken up the unfinished score and completed the First Symphony at the age when he actually wrote the Ninth. And though, as we shall see, it is possible to make a fairly definite conjecture as to the point where the join occurs in the first movement, there is no such stylistic clash as we should expect to find in a work completed after a considerable interval by a persistently active composer. The style of the sixty-year-old Balakirev is so like that of the thirty-year-old (already fairly mature) that, considering the completely unconventional form of the first movement, one would never suspect the truth but for Rimsky-Korsakov's casual remark.

The first movement, however completed, is a very remarkable one; indeed in several respects unique. Its completely unconventional architecture may be accounted for in part by that thirty years' interval, but only in part. In the last century such formal freedom usually invited a surmise that a "programme" must be at the bottom of it: "We cannot make head or tail of it, so we suppose it must be a symphonic poem," as a bewildered or sarcastic critic said of the corresponding movement in Brahms's C minor. But there is no reason to suppose anything of the sort in this case. The architecture of the movement appears chaotic when judged by any familiar conventional standard. Yet its form is perfect, in the sense that the "form" of one of the best of the "Forty-eight" Fugues or of the "Siegfried Idyll" is perfect, since it arises spontaneously from the content. It is spun not from two main themes but from one theme, itself dual in nature; and this theme, though continually transformed in the Lisztian manner, can hardly be said to flower like a theme of Beethoven's. But the composer's exuberantly fertile imagination continually playing with it, weaves from it and about it a continuous web of sound, the natural unrolling of which *is* the form of the movement. There are occasional references to passages heard before, but never repetitions of whole stretches of music; only enough to show that the composer, though he keeps marching ahead, has not forgotten the scenery he passed just now. And except for a curious *fugato* episode, there is hardly a bar not derived directly or indirectly from the parent theme. Such a close-knit musical argument, so long sustained and so eloquently expressed by a master-orchestrator, would make this movement one of the finest in the whole range of symphonic literature if its qualities were not partially off-set by certain defects in both the orator and his subject. Balakirev's argument does not march clearly and

inevitably. Like the man himself, it is freakish.
The chain of logic is perfect but the links are unequal in strength. But the marvel is that he is able
to say so much of such importance on such a subject, and to say it with such passion and eloquence.
Here is the gist of the thing, as it is stated in the
opening bars of the slow introduction:

Neither part of it, *a* nor *b*, promises much; *a*, having no rhythmic vitality, plays a nearly passive rôle
throughout, like one of Dickens's youthful heroes.
Its function as the nucleus of the whole keeps it
to the fore; it is the predominating motive; but it is
b that is the vitalising agent. The rich fulfilment
of the movement far exceeds the slender promise
of the theme, but all Balakirev's exuberance—a
threefold exuberance, physical, intellectual and imaginative—cannot quite disguise the inadequacy of
the material on which it works.

The slow prologue modulates incessantly, as does the whole movement that follows. That is another of Balakirev's idiosyncrasies, thoroughly characteristic of his nervous, restless temperament. (And nothing could be more curious than the constant tendency of his music, no matter what its nominal key, to drift toward D or D flat or the relative minors.) This *largo*, in essence one long-drawn crescendo, breaks into an energetic *allegro vivo* in 2-4 time. Ex. 63*a* (in quavers) makes a poor first subject, but Ex. 63*b* as the second already begins to show its mettle.*. In its new form it provides the text for a vigorous and tightly-woven piece of musical argument. This 2-4 passage lasts for 164 bars, when the time signature changes to 2-2 (in which it remains for the rest of the movement) and the opening of the *allegro* is now played by the lower strings *pizzicato* in notes of double value:

in which form it is far more effective. And here, I suspect, at this double bar or just before or after it, is where Balakirev laid down his pen in the 'sixties. Whether the 2-2 continuation was part of the composer's original plan, it is difficult to say. On the whole, I am inclined to think he started it and aban-

---
* See Ex. 89 in my "Studies in Russian Music."

doned it after twenty bars or so. But of course it is possible that the 2-2 was an entirely new idea when the composer took up the score again, and that the last twelve bars of the 2-4, harking back to the end of the *largo*, were devised later to disguise the change of signature, as they effectually do. As it stands, this 2-4 passage seems to fall naturally into place in the scheme of the movement as a whole, yet it is fairly clear, on the evidence of the different treatment of the material here from that in the rest of the movement, that this was the "about a third" which Korsakov saw scored in the sixties. The rest of the movement, finely wrought as it is, has not the same terse vigour; though no one, I think, would notice the fact unless he had been warned to look for something of the sort. A wealth of music type would be needed to show the infinite subtleties of this movement, the gradual revelation of the intimate relationship of Ex. 63a and b, the harking back to past episodes, apparently transient and unimportant, and the demonstration of their indispensability to the whole scheme—in short, the things that make music "symphonic" in the truest sense. But it is necessary to emphasise that they *are* present in this movement. Western musicians have a regrettable tendency to judge Russian symphonic music hastily and superficially by its more obvious attractions; perhaps because the best known of Russian symphonists has so little else to offer. And this careless standard of judgment, apparently so much more lenient than that we apply to the great German classics, is actually if not a more severe, a more unfair test. It would be perfectly natural for even an attentive listener, hearing this piece for the first time, to find in it little more than a *mélange* of attractive ideas, beautifully orchestrated and repeatedly whipped up into exciting climaxes. Unless we study Balakirev's scores as closely as we do Brahms's, we can hardly hope to find in them any equivalent of the enduring qualities that make Brahms's what they are. Russian music has been to a great extent the victim of its own *Klangreiz* (I can find no English equivalent for Joachim's expressive word); though as Balakirev's symphonies are scarcely played at all, it might be said that it is hardly true in his case. Yet conductors evidently prefer the exotic, sensuous charm of "Tamara" to the less obvious qualities of the symphonies.

The scherzo again is not obviously effective, like the scherzi of Tchaïkovsky's Fourth and Borodin's Second. But it grows on one, and even at a first hearing one easily succumbs to the fascination of the trio melody, apparently in the Æolian mode but in a context that suggests the Dorian. Incidentally, this scherzo is not the one originally intended for the symphony. Balakirev worked up the sketches of the original scherzo later in his Second Symphony.

Balakirev's Symphonies.

With the last two movements we get back to the more familiar ground of obvious Russianness. But they are such extraordinarily good specimens of their kind, especially the finale, that one would have thought that these alone would win the symphony at least an occasional performance. The slow movement is one of those languorous nocturnes, sensuously rather than sentimentally sweet, of which the older Russians were so fond. It is based on a typically Balakirevian clarinet melody, long drawn and consisting essentially of little more than a single note decorated with arabesques.

The whole *andante* is in the same quasi-oriental vein—this is the Balakirev of "Tamara"—and finally fades through a harp cadenza into the exceedingly virile finale, a movement as physically and mentally bracing as its predecessor is enervating. There are three subjects. The opening one is a real peasant tune; it is No. 40 of Rimsky-Korsakov's "Hundred Russian Folk-Songs":

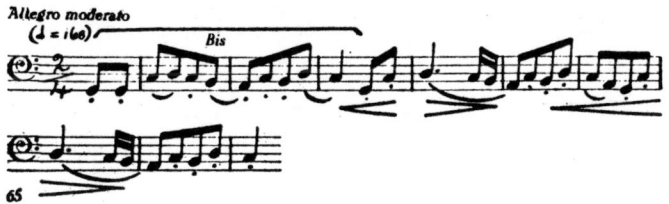

The second, hardly more than a rhythm,

188   *On Russian Music.*

is of oriental origin. According to K. Chernov, Balakirev heard this tune when travelling third class on the Finnish Railway on one occasion. An old blind man boarded the train and "began to sing in a loud voice, accompanying himself on a primitive, fearfully out-of-tune harp," afterwards passing round the hat. Ex. 66 was one of the old man's tunes; it caught Balakirev's fancy and he made a note of it. The third theme of the finale is full of rhythmic "punch":*

---

* Rimsky-Korsakov speaks of Ex. 65 as the first subject of the

(The final motive x is very characteristic of Balakirev.) It will be noticed that many of Balakirev's most characteristic themes are marked by movement from a strong beat, instead of toward one. Bars one and three of Ex. 64, for instance, are "strong" bars and the whole effect of the theme would be weakened by following the (expressive, not metrical) inflection of the opening (Ex. 63) and making them weak ones. When a little later in this passage the composer wants the accent shifted from the "odd" to the "even" bars, he is careful to mark it. Balakirev's themes also acquire electrifying rhythmic energy from unexpected subdivisions of the beat, either in the accompaniment or in the melody itself. In this movement the whirling triplets of Ex. 66 are first contrasted with the sturdy 2-4 of Ex. 65 and then driven against it, side by side. The whole of the finale is a masterly demonstration of the symphonic possibilities of rhythm. And the crowning touch comes at the end when the apparently runaway steed is superbly reined in and the time pulled back for a few final bars in *tempo di polacca*. Here again is a piece of genuine symphonic feeling, for the value of this polonaise coda, based on a metamorphosis of Ex. 65, depends almost entirely on what has gone before.

The Second Symphony in D minor, dedicated

---

finale as originally planned, but says that the second subject was one of the "millet-sowing ritual" songs in Balakirev's published collection of folk-songs. There is no trace of this in the definitive version of the movement.

to the memory of that A. D. Ulibishev who was Mozart's biographer and Balakirev's benefactor, was completed early in 1908, only a year or so before the composer's death. Here we find a first movement much more conventional in design (though not in key scheme) than that of the earlier work. But the work is more supple, more highly charged with inward vitality. Everything bespeaks the confident master—the curt opening chords, the authority of the chief subject, and the impetuous course of the music, music as urgently alive, as free from padding and artificiality on the one hand and non-musical excitement on the other, as anything in the whole range of Russian music. The crossing of 3-4 and 6-8, hinted at in the opening theme, is emphasised in the unfolding of the second subject, which again owes everything to its rhythmic features, as natural as they are original. This movement presents no such difficulties as the corresponding one in the C major Symphony. Everything is clear and immediately effective. It never leaves earth for heaven, but it does carry absolute conviction that Balakirev felt it was bliss to be alive even at seventy. The curt, masterful ending of the movement, surprising without being sensational, reminds one of Sibelius.

The "Scherzo alla Cosacca" (originally intended for the first Symphony, as we have seen) is Balakirev at his most brilliant. Even the naïve little folk-tune (No. 33 of Korsakov's "Hundred

Folk Songs") which is the basis of the trio, is soon caught up into the general excitement. Borrowed folk-tunes, and there are a good many of them, play a peculiar part in Balakirev's music. He does not penetrate to the heart of them, subtly bringing out and magnifying their latent significance. Nor does he deck them out in gorgeous and thoroughly unsuitable orchestral fancy dress. But a given folk-song seems to have the effect of exciting his creative imagination to play around it, very much as a literary essayist is set going by almost any trivial topic that happens to come along. Like the born essayist's subjects, Balakirev's borrowed folk-tunes are little more than the keys which unlock his exuberant fancy.

As in the First Symphony, so in the Second, the slow movement is the weakest. It is headed "Romanza," and that indicates the nature of its weakness; it is not very strong in itself and seems quite out of place in a symphony predominately epic and heroic in character. But in the finale Balakirev returns to the most heroic of dance measures, the polonaise. And this is no such conventional polonaise, showy and blatant, as we get from Tchaïkovsky (Third Symphony; Suite in G, etc.), Rimsky-Korsakov ("Christmas Eve") and Mussorgsky ("Boris"). Balakirev is concerned more with the spirit than the form of the dance. Brilliant it certainly is, brilliant even for Balakirev, but the brilliance is only one of the outward signs of intense inward excitement. It never deteriorates into mere empty glitter. The opening theme is another of those typically Balakirevian melodies, seemingly packed to bursting-point with concentrated energy; and as usual the illusion of "knotted muscles" is traceable to the unusual subdivisions of the rhythm. The second subject, again a folk-song (No. 31 in the Rimsky-Korsakov collection), is underlined with the characteristic accompanying rhythm of the second subject of the first movement (though now of course in 3-4 instead of 6-8 time). And with this jolly Russian dance tune disappears the last shadow of a suspicion of pseudo-Polishness in the movement; though as a matter of fact even the opening is no more Polish in spirit than Chopin's waltzes are Austrian. The chivalric spirit of the polonaise naturally appealed to a composer concerned with the heroic as persistently as Balakirev was. So whereas the polonaise was to Glinka and Mussorgsky a symbol for the alien and hostile, and to Tchaïkovsky and Korsakov merely a dance form of no particular significance at all, Balakirev broke into a final *tempo di polacca* for his "happy ending" as naturally as Bach and his contemporaries let off their final high spirits in a gigue.

XV.—BALAKIREV'S MUSIC TO "KING LEAR."

In the middle of the last century the existence of a vast treasure-store of English folk-music was almost unknown, and the little that was known was undervalued. True, William Chappell had published his "Collection of National English Airs" (1838-40), afterwards enlarged and re-titled "Popular Music of the Olden Time," but no English composer of the period would have thought of using an English folk-tune as the basis of an instrumental composition. To find an example of that we must look much further afield—to Russia. In the late 1850's Balakirev was using an English folk-song as no English composer thought of doing till forty years later. The story is interesting for its own sake and, in addition, the telling of it may help to draw attention to one of the acknowledged masterpieces of Russian music, a work that remains practically unknown in England: Balakirev's overture and incidental music to "King Lear."

The critic, Vladimir Stassov, like the majority of cultured Russians of the period after the Crimean

War, was an Anglophile. Not only that, but he was connected by marriage with an English family named Clark, owners of a well-known Petersburg iron foundry. His gods were Byron, Shakespeare and Beethoven, and his Shakespeare-worship was the immediate cause of more than one Shakespearean composition (e.g., Tchaïkovsky's "Tempest" and "Romeo and Juliet"). In July, 1858, we find Stassov writing to the twenty-year-old Balakirev:

"I should like above all to know whether you are sticking to your intention to write music for 'Lear' and, if so, whether entr'actes and overture or just an overture only? and if you have actually started on all this, whether it is going well, and *how* and *what?* I ask you this because I should like to pass on the story officially to the Directors of the Imperial Theatres. . . . If you can tell me that everything is going well with you, I should think I could send in a paper or note to the Theatre Committee, which is now busy with the mounting of 'Lear' [at the Alexandrinsky Theatre, Petersburg], saying that music is now being prepared *on such-and-such lines*, which it would be as well for them to consider. Apropos of 'Lear,' here is another *very old* English song for you,* to the music of which the English peasants in Gloucestershire to this very day sing a sort of ballad

---

* Evidently Stassov had given Balakirev some English melodies when the idea of writing music to "Lear" had first occurred to him. Presumably Ex. 73 below was one of these.

about the Anglo-Norman [sic] invasion of England, in an old English dialect which it is now almost impossible to make out:

68

Good, isn't it? And here also is a *fool's song* for you from Shakespeare's 'Twelfth Night.' This is the actual music used for this on the English stage in the lifetime of Shakespeare himself :*

69

A German writer on music, who quotes this song in a musical paper, says that Mendelssohn probably came across it when he was in England and used it in his 'Midsummer Night's Dream' to depict the peasant clowns:

70

---

* I give Exs. 69 and 71 in abbreviated form.

In Shakespeare's lifetime they used this music for the chorus of elves in 'A Midsummer Night's Dream'—I hope you'll like it:

71

There's some pretty *genuine* English music for you. I hope that from these and the earlier ones you'll be able to choose something that will be of use to you."

One interesting point is proved by Stassov's first two quotations: that the Russian critic knew the first volume of Chappell's "Popular Music of the Olden Time," published in 1855 (the second volume did not appear till 1859). For both quotations are identical in notation, key, etc., with Chappell's versions. The first tune is "Oh, ponder well"; it exists with various sets of words, including the verses, "When Arthur first in court began" (mentioned by Falstaff in "Henry IV"), and Stassov, never very accurate, evidently took King Arthur for an "Anglo-Norman" king. As for the second melody, Chappell says that the tune has no authority other than theatrical tradition for being accepted as the original music for "When that I was and a little tiny boy." But he points out something that Stassov curiously does not tell Balakirev: that the Fool in "King Lear" has a song, "He that has and a little tiny wit," with the same "Hey, ho, the wind and the rain" burden, which fits the tune equally well.

Detained in distant Nizhny-Novgorod and for various reasons thoroughly out of spirits, Balakirev replied a week later:

"'King Lear' is now at a standstill. The last entr'acte is begun and only a few bars are wanting to finish it. But probably nothing more will get written during the summer. I don't even think about music at all.... To write in Nizhny in these circumstances is impossible. In any case, it will be impossible to finish by September. I always spend a long time pondering over things. Remember that I began to write the Russian Overture* in November, 1857, and ended it only in June. And of course it was incomparably easier to write than music to 'Lear,' as in that case I was subject only to myself, while here I've had to subject myself to Shakespeare and so carry out a *difficult* task. The longer I take, the better it will be, and if the [theatre] directorate doesn't accept my music, it won't matter very much; if it gets done a couple of times at the University I shall be satisfied. I wouldn't write the overture alone *for the world*, although the all-wise directorate promised me money for it. I must tell you that *I'm very* pleased with the last entr'acte and I see now that, if I manage to write all the entr'actes *well*, the overture

---

* Overture on Three Russian Themes.

may *easily* turn out *first-rate*. . . . For the present they can use Berlioz's music or, if not that, Kazhinsky himself [the conductor of the Alexandrinsky Theatre] composes; such music would be more suitable for the Alexandrinsky Theatre than mine; I don't think much of the public of the University concerts, still less of that of the Alexandrinsky. Thank you for the English themes. I will give them most careful thought. Meanwhile, could you let me know where the Fool has to sing and in what places Shakespeare himself had music?"

Actually, the overture was composed by the end of the year (1858),* and orchestrated (according to a note on the manuscript score) "September 13th-18th, 1859—6.30 in the evening." It was rehearsed and played for the first time a month or two later, and was at once generally accepted as one of the outstanding works of the "new Russian school." (It was through this piece that the sixteen-year-old Rimsky-Korsakov made Balakirev's acquaintance in 1860). But it appears from a further letter of Stassov's that two entr'actes still remained to be done in January, 1860. And in February, 1861, the composer writes: "How glad I shall be when I manage to finish the last thing for 'Lear.'" Then

---

* Years later, Balakirev described at great length to Tchaïkovsky the way in which he devised the overture. The letter, translated in the English edition of "Tchaïkovsky's Life and Letters" and again in my own "Studies in Russian Music," need not be quoted here.

four days later, at midnight, he scribbles a hasty note :

"Have just finished the 'Procession' [i.e., the entry of the court in Act I, after Gloster's words : 'The king is coming.'] It only remains to orchestrate it. That's easy. You won't believe how glad I am. Now enough of worrying about 'Lear.' You say that there's still something to be done to it—but there isn't; I've expended on the 'Procession' all that I still had in my head for 'Lear.' How glad I am that it's finished, and at the same time sorry that I haven't got to think about 'Lear' any more. My head has become so weak, my brain aches, my feet are as cold as ice, a sort of nervous shivering has seized me. Yesterday I thought to such a degree (I was composing the 'Procession') that there was a moment when I fancied I should go out of my mind."

The whole of the "King Lear" music was thus finished in 1861, the overture as early as 1859. The overture, at least, was performed frequently. But Balakirev was not quite satisfied with his work; he wished to revise it thoroughly, and so withheld it from publication. But the revision was constantly postponed and this work, which Russian critics compare with Schumann's "Manfred" music and even with Beethoven's "Egmont," had to wait till 1904 before it was printed.

To write music to "King Lear" is as daring a challenge as any a composer can issue. Berlioz and

Balakirev are almost the only composers who have ventured it; Debussy merely touched the fringe of the subject and then drew back nervously. Even Verdi fought shy of it. Berlioz's overture is a fine piece of work, too seldom heard, but only a very fanatical Berliozian would consider it worthy of Shakespeare. And Balakirev's overture? To assert that it is on the plane of Shakespeare's tragedy would be absurd. But it is hardly going too far to claim that it is the most satisfactory interpretation of the tragic side of Shakespeare yet made in terms of music, at least as adequate as Mendelssohn's transmutation of "A Midsummer Night's Dream." The opening of the *allegro moderato*, presenting at once the two chief themes associated with Lear himself (*a* and *b*) and the theme of the cruel daughters (*c*), takes one nearer the world of the great German classics than almost anything else in Russian music (Ex. 72).

The introduction is striking enough: answering fanfares on brass and drums, suggesting curious overlappings of keys—a chivalrous major version of Ex. 72*a*—then another, slow version of Ex. 72*a* on the wind ("something mystical," as the composer spoke of it to Tchaïkovsky)—"Kent's prediction" on the horns. But it is only with the main *allegro moderato* that the music rises to something approaching the Shakespearean level. This great passionate *allegro*, relieved only by the gracious theme of Cordelia (the orthodox second subject), is

curiously classical in feeling: stern, clear-cut, remarkably free from the harmonic and melodic lusciousness characteristic of Russian romanticism. Only one trace of romanticism remains—the "storm" that constitutes the development section; and it is probably the most restrained storm in the whole of nineteenth century music, suggesting the tempest in Lear's unhappy mind, rather than an actual, physical storm.

The rest of the music, if hardly on the level of the overture, is no less interesting. Besides one or two short numbers (e.g., nineteen bars of the "Cordelia" music after Kent's "Fortune, good-night: smile once more; turn thy wheel," as he goes to sleep) and numerous fanfares, it consists of processional music for the entry of the court in Act I, and preludes to Acts II, III, IV and V. There is no vocal music, but a brief passage of "melodrama" occurs in the music for Act V, Scene 2.

The "Procession" is a brilliant polonaise for double orchestra—ordinary full orchestra and a band of wind, brass and percussion behind the scenes (later on the stage)—though there is an alternative version for normal orchestra alone. The opening is identical with the opening of the overture, and the answering fanfares gain much in effectiveness by the distribution of the instruments. The trio is amusingly Russian in feeling, the piece as a whole very imposing in a superficial way. (However, Stassov considered it "the best of the entr'actes, though not better than the overture.") Nor are the preludes to Acts II and V of great importance. The first is a musical portrait of Goneril and Regan, based on their characteristic themes in the overture. The second rather perfunctorily sketches "The Battle—Lear's Death by Cordelia's Body—Apotheosis"; it is less interest-

Balakirev's *Music to "King Lear."*

ing than the music accompanying the "alarums" in Scene 2 (again with a brass band on the stage) and Edgar's "Here, father, take the shadow of this tree."

The prelude to Act III (or rather to the second scene—Balakirev directs that Scene 1 must be omitted) is a much better piece of work. Beginning with a fine, gloomy tone picture of the heath (on Lear's theme, Ex. 72*b*), interspersed with two references to the fool's theme, Ex. 69, it passes into the storm music of the overture, which dies away as the curtain goes up and Lear and his companion cross the stage. But the gem of the whole set of entr'actes is the prelude to Act IV, extraordinarily interesting in that it is based almost entirely on the "thème anglais":

and a very lovely piece of music into the bargain. Ex. 73 is first stated by the cor anglais unaccompanied and then treated as the theme of a set of "changing background" variations, more or less anticipating Delius's method in "Brigg Fair," the variations being only twice interrupted by references to the "Lear" and "Cordelia" themes. The harmonisation is always simple and sympathetically wistful, the scoring extraordinarily delicate and subtly tinted. (The influence of Berlioz is very obvious.) Nor has Balakirev finished with his "English theme" even now. In Act IV, Scene 7, after the physician's command: "Louder the music there!" it is played by musicians on the stage (flute, cor anglais, clarinets, bassoons and harp)—an exquisite miniature of just twenty-six bars.

XVI.—BALAKIREV'S PIANO SONATA.

The parallel between Liszt and Balakirev is close enough to attract the attention of the most superficial observer. Both were remarkable pianists; both had dominating personalities which naturally made them leaders in great progressive musical movements, and the champions of men with greater creative gifts than their own; both were keenly interested in folk music and drew on it heavily in their own compositions; both died at nearly the same age—seventy-four. As composers, both left, in addition to a number of unjustly neglected orchestral works, a great deal of very difficult, rather showy piano music, including a large proportion of transcriptions—and each wrote a single piano sonata of strikingly unconventional design. The Liszt sonata is, of course, often heard, and its design—one big movement in orthodox sonata form, containing all the emotional elements of the normal four movements—has been accepted as a pattern by various modern writers, notably by Arnold Bax in his own piano sonatas. But there seems to be a conspiracy of silence against Balakirev's B flat minor work (published in 1905). Rosa Newmarch, in her article on Balakirev in the last edition of "Grove," omits all mention of it, and of the Concerto in E flat, Balakirev's last composition. An article on the composer which appeared some years ago in a paper the majority of whose readers are piano teachers (whom one would naturally expect to be particularly interested in Balakirev's most important piano work), followed Mrs. Newmarch's omissions and inaccuracies even to the extent of saying that "he wrote only one symphony." Nor does Montagu-Nathan mention the sonata in his "History of Russian Music," though he speaks of the concerto and the second symphony.

Nothing could show more graphically the appalling neglect that befell Balakirev in his last years. Russia took so little notice of the compositions of his last period that foreigners did not even know they existed.

The Sonata is dedicated to Lyapunov, of all Balakirev's pupils the one who was most intimately associated with him personally and who followed most closely in his footsteps as a composer. Apparently less unconventional than the Liszt work, it proves on examination to be much more so. Indeed, its four movements—*andantino, mazurka,* and *intermezzo* (a four-page *larghetto*) leading without a break into the final *allegro non troppo, ma con fuoco*—suggest that the work is a suite rather than a sonata. This question of mere nomenclature is not quite so unimportant as it may appear to be. When Dvorák complained that Tchaïkovsky's symphonies were really suites, he was not exhibiting academic narrow-mindedness, but making a perfectly legitimate criticism of Tchaïkovsky's architectural weaknesses in an easily understandable way. We know perfectly well what he meant: not that Tchaïkovsky had called his works by a name he had no right to give them, but that the individual movements, instead of being four wings of one building, were four separate buildings grouped together to look like one. Everyone must feel that the movements of the E minor Symphony, in spite of the motto-theme with which the composer tried to rubber-stamp them as belonging to each other, are not related as the movements of Mozart's G minor Symphony, for instance, are related to each other. The relationship of the Mozart movements could hardly be demonstrated, but we *feel* it none the less strongly—and in such cases feeling (if we are confident that our taste is sound) is a surer guide than intellectual deduction from definite and tangible evidence. On playing the Balakirev Sonata, one's first impression is that the thing is not a homogeneous whole; but that impression has very soon to be revised. Balakirev does not try to impose an artificial unity on his work by factitious means such as Tchaïkovsky uses, though it is true he harks back, in the middle of the finale, to the intermezzo. But the episode is so handled that one is hardly conscious that a quotation is being made, although it is actually a "verbatim" one; it seems to have a natural place at just that point in the tissue of the music. Yet, with the possible exception of the second movement, which does seem a little excrescent—more in the nature of an intermezzo than the movement actually so called—the material of the whole Sonata, except the mazurka, evidently emanated from the same heat of imagination. Searching for thematic resemblances, in confirmation of this view, one can certainly find them; but they are so slight and so subtle as to make it appear highly improbable that they were the result of conscious manipulation on the lines of Liszt's metamorphoses of themes. The virile and ruthless opening subject of the finale:

later begets another, a feminine counterpart of itself, yet obviously related to it only by a single fragmentary motive:

Again, this "feminine counterpart" undergoes a change which seems to relate it to part of the subject of the first movement (cf. Ex. 77x):

and then melts imperceptibly into the quotation from the intermezzo already referred to.

The extraordinary first movement contains the germs of all these cells of musical thought. Its plan is unique, though Mozart and others have toyed with the underlying idea—the reconciliation of the fugue with sonata-form. The subject is a long one, eight bars in very moderate *tempo*, a beautiful piece of *cantilena*, characteristically Russian in its arabesque twists and curves.

The orthodox fugal exposition comes to a full close in D flat, and from this cadence springs, in the most natural way, a little transition theme, over a simple arpeggio bass; it is only two bars long but with each repetition it spreads its petals wider till it flowers into sweeping arpeggios against which the fugue theme sings out in the tenor. The music rises to a climax with the fugue theme in canon, and then dies away to nothing. This section corresponds to the "exposition" of ordinary sonata-form, and there are few finer examples in existence of what Ernest Newman has described as "music unfolding itself in obedience to the inner laws of its own being." A horn-like D flat is heard alone and the development begins in G flat minor (written enharmonically as F sharp minor). This is to all intents and purposes a free *stretto*, for the most part with two contrapuntal voices supported by widespread left-hand arpeggios, culminating in a rhapsodic cadenza. The recapitulation follows in due course, but with this difference—that the music breaks off just before the peak of the big climax is reached, and a bitter-sweet coda follows, quietly brooding over the theme and showing it in a fresh light. So much for the skeleton of the movement: it is unfortunate that one cannot speak of the design of a piece of music without giving the impression that one has been talking about nothing but dry bones. But only in this way is it possible to give any idea of the nature of Balakirev's brilliant experiment.

The notion that music can entirely evolve its own form "in obedience to the inner laws of its own being" is, of course, absurd. Every art-work must to some extent accept some sort of design imposed on it from without. That is one of the conditions of the artist's problem, which is simply to find a compromise between his ideas in the raw state and a number of limitations of every kind from those of order and design to those laid on him by the fact of ten fingers and the nature of the sounds produced by striking a wire with a hammer (in the case of a piano composer). How far the artist takes these limitations into consideration is a matter that concerns no one but himself : he may pay great heed to some and little to others. But he disregards them at his peril. The greatest artists have generally been those who have shown the greatest respect for the peculiar nature of their medium, that is, for its limitations. And the painter, though he has a perfect right to reject a rectangular boundary to his picture, must nevertheless limit it somehow, must accept some sort of shape imposed on it from without. To the musician the problem of outline naturally presents itself in a different guise. The *limits* of his work are merely a matter of time, but its *shape* must be based on some convention—unless the music is to straggle aimlessly. "But music should unfold itself organically, not be fitted into a framework." Granted. But music, like other organisms, needs a framework to guide its development, and as it does not grow a natural one, as the vertebrate mammals do, it must be provided with an artificial one, such as we give rambler roses. The ideal framework is that which perfectly suits the particular organism. In this first movement of his Sonata, Balakirev has imposed on his predominantly fugal organism only enough of the broad outline of sonata-form to give it definite shape. How far he has succeeded in this and in the fusion of harmonic and contrapuntal elements is, of course, a matter for personal opinion to decide, but even if the complete success of the experiment is open to question, its interest is undeniable.

It might be objected that the mazurka which follows is too long and perhaps too slight in material to be quite in focus with the rest of the work, yet the flavour of its themes gives it extraordinary charm as a self-contained piece. (It was indeed written before the rest of the Sonata, as an independent composition.) And the handling of the material is as characteristically Russian as the material itself—little development, but much repetition of themes against fresh and striking backgrounds. The intermezzo is thoughtful, enigmatic, rather austere in its simplicity, and the fiery finale, with all its barbaric exuberance, ends in a similar mood. But in discussing Balakirev's work it is perhaps better to avoid speaking of "moods" or of anything savouring, however slightly, of an emotional programme, for the stuff of his compositions is so purely musical that one listens to them without any thought of extra-musical elements. And this in spite of the fact that Balakirev so often adopted a programmatic basis for his music. For, except possibly in "Tamara," the programme was with Balakirev merely a pretext, the necessary framework *not* arising directly from his material, which he adopted as another composer might have adopted sonata-form or rondo-form.

It is hardly necessary to say that the Sonata is perfectly conceived in terms of its medium; for, unlike the piano-music of the other Russian masters, Skryabin excepted, everything Balakirev wrote for the instrument is peculiarly *Klaviermässig*. That is to say, in spite of its difficulty (though nothing like that of "Islamey") and occasional awkwardness for the hands, even the melodic lines are almost all conceived for a percussion instrument, an instrument whose tone begins to die directly it is born. So Balakirev writes melodies more like strings of pearls or diamonds than silken threads. Sometimes, as in "Islamey," he exploits the percussive possibilities of the instrument even more fully, and in the second movement he is so resourceful of device that he almost tricks us into accepting purely pianistic effects as substitutes for orchetral colour—though not, of course, by "turning the piano into a full orchestra" in the sense that Brahms has been reproached with doing. Widespread left-hand arpeggio figures, often distributed over nearly three octaves, are striking features of all four movements. Balakirev always had a predilection for well-spread left-hand writing, but in this Sonata he employs it so fully that one cannot help wondering whether he had taken a hint from Skryabin.

But the Sonata is as pure an expression of Balakirev's striking personality as he ever gave the world: that is, of his musical personality, for the element of subjective expression is practically non-existent in Balakirev's compositions. His individuality manifests itself here, as always in his music, simply in the workings of his musical intelligence. And we must remember that the moments of apparent affinity with Borodin and Korsakov in the second and fourth movements are not to be taken as evidence of the influence of those composers. Rather the reverse. Balakirev is only recovering old debts, for these elements were either drawn from the common stock of folk-song or actually originated with himself. The question of the extent of Balakirev's influence on the other members of the "mighty handful" has not yet been fully investigated, and it is possible that we never shall be able to determine it precisely. But there can be no doubt that Borodin, and Rimsky-Korsakov to an even greater extent, were far more heavily indebted to Balakirev than is generally realised. Yet in his work he stands curiously aloof from them, except in the common sphere of the orchestra, for whereas they were both strongly attracted by the theatre, Balakirev avoided it altogether, and while their music for piano is negligible in both quantity and quality, the instrument was, next to the orchestra, his favourite medium of expression. His Sonata has, therefore, the distinction of being the only large-scale piano composition produced by the group of Russian nationalist composers, if we except Mussorgsky's " Pictures from an Exhibition," a suite which must be regarded as music conceived as abstract sound and written down for the piano, rather than as genuine piano music.

XVII.—"THE FAIR OF SOROCHINTSY" AND CHEREPNIN'S COMPLETION OF IT.

Of all Russian writers, Mussorgsky's favourite was always Gogol. As early as 1858 he had thought of basing an opera on Gogol's story, "St. John's Eve," and it is possible that the "witches' sabbath" music known to us in Rimsky-Korsakov's scoring as "Night on the Bare Mountain" was originally written for this projected opera. But that is only surmise. Ten years later, as everyone knows, Mussorgsky actually began a setting of Gogol's prose comedy, "The Marriage," an extraordinarily interesting experiment in "dramatic truth," of which only one act was completed. But his attention seems to have been first turned to "The Fair of Sorochintsy" by Nadezhda Purgold (afterwards Rimsky-Korsakov's wife).

Both Nadezhda and her fiancé were extremely fond of Gogol's "Evenings on a Farm near Dikanka" (the collection of tales which includes

"The Fair"). In December, 1871, she wrote to her lover: "I've been reading yet another of Gogol's stories to-day, 'The Fair of Sorochintsy.'* This is good, too, and would even be suitable for an opera, but not for you; in any case, it's not like 'May Night.'" Either she or her sister Alexandra then appears to have suggested to Mussorgsky that he should compose an opera on "The Fair," but he replied (January 3rd/15th, 1872): "I know the Gogol subject very well, in fact I thought about it a couple of years ago, but it does not fit in with the line I have chosen for myself." Two years later he changed his mind, writing to Lyubov Karmalina (July 23rd/August 4th, 1874) that he is embarking on "a comic opera, 'The Fair of Sorochintsy,' after Gogol," as light relief from his "two heavyweights, 'Boris' and 'Khovanshchina'": "The materials of Ukrainian folk-song are so little known that lay connoisseurs look upon them as imitations (of what?) dug up wholesale. In short, there's any amount of stuff to draw on." According to Stassov, the immediate impulse was the idea of writing an

---

* Gogol's story is little more than a farcical anecdote, brilliantly told: Parasya, the daughter of a stupid old peasant, falls in love at the fair with a *parabok* (young peasant) named Gritsko. True love meets with the usual difficulties, which are removed by a shrewd but kindly gypsy who exposes the love-affair of Cherevik's wife, Khivrya, with a priest's son, Afanasy Ivanovich—and who incidentally takes advantage of a popular legend of a "devil in a red jacket" to play on the superstitious fears of the other characters at critical moments.

Ukrainian part for the great Ukrainian bass, O. A. Petrov.

Mussorgsky was in the middle of the composition of "Khovanshchina" and throughout the remaining seven years of his unhappy drunken life he struggled fitfully at the composition of both operas instead of concentrating on one, with the result that he left both unfinished. "The Fair" was a muddle from the beginning, for Mussorgsky had no proper libretto and even the scenario for the first and third acts was not put on paper till May, 1877. As in "Boris," Mussorgsky proposed to use music salvaged from earlier works: the "Bare Mountain" music, the "Mlada" of 1872, and so on. But deepening interest in "Khovanshchina" thrust "The Fair" on one side, and in April, 1875, he announced to Lyubov Karmalina that he had "given up the Little Russian [i.e., Ukrainian] opera," owing to "the impossibility of a Great Russian's pretending to be a Little Russian, and consequently the impossibility of mastering Little Russian recitative, all the nuances and peculiarities of the musical rise and fall of Little Russian speech." Nevertheless in the summer of 1876, probably jogged into activity by the celebration of Petrov's artistic jubilee in April, he took up "The Fair" again and worked hard at both that and "Khovanshchina."

The summer of the following year was also dedicated to the Gogol opera, and at last Mussorgsky drew up a scenario (dated "May 19th, 1877, at the

Petrovs'"). But in November Stassov wrote to Golenishchev-Kutuzov that "Mussorgsky has written a lot of rubbish for 'The Fair of Sorochintsy' this summer, but has now decided to throw it all away. . . . During the last few weeks he has written a couple of gypsy choruses (also for 'The Fair')." But Petrov died in March, 1878, and we hear no more of "The Fair" till February, 1880, when Stassov reported to Balakirev that "some people are helping Mussorgsky at the rate of eighty rubles a month on condition that he finishes his 'Fair of Sorochintsy' within about a year." (Unfortunately another group of friends had already offered him a rather bigger pension to finish "Khovanshchina"—and he tried to earn both.) However the backers of "The Fair" induced him to arrange some excerpts* from it as piano solos and to sell them to the publisher Bernard. Towards the end of August, 1880, Mussorgsky was able to inform Stassov that he had "perpetrated the Fair Scene." And there apparently he left the work. Paul Lamm published the torso as the composer left it but completed by Shebalin in 1933.

Like Mussorgsky's other and more important operas, "The Fair" has had an adventurous posthumous history. Rimsky-Korsakov left it alone, but other hands have been only too willing to pre-

---

* The popular little "Hopak," Khivrya's song, Parasya's song, and the scene between Afanasy Ivanovich and Khivrya.

pare "performing versions" from Mussorgsky's sketches. There are five versions in all:

1. Mussorgsky's fragments, edited by the critic V. G. Karatïgin and partly orchestrated by Lyadov, were published in 1912 by Bessel. These fragments had already been performed in Petersburg, once privately and once in public, the previous year.

2. In 1913, a version of these fragments arranged and orchestrated by Sakhnovsky, with the missing scenes given in spoken dialogue, was performed at the Moscow Free Theatre.

3. In 1915, the eighty-year-old Cui completed the score and produced a version performed in Petersburg in October, 1917, just a week before the outbreak of the Bolshevist Revolution. Cui's version was published by Bessel in 1924.

4. Just after the War, N. N. Cherepnin, an ex-pupil of Rimsky-Korsakov's, living in exile in Paris, completed and orchestrated the work; his version was produced at Monte Carlo in March, 1923, and also published by Bessel in 1924.*

5. The already mentioned edition prepared from the original manuscripts by Paul Lamm, with additions by Shebalin, and issued by the Russian State Publishing Company in 1933.

It was the fourth version which was produced at Covent Garden on November 24th, 1936. Whereas Cui preserved the plan outlined in Mussorgsky's

---

* With a preface by Louis Laloy, containing more inaccuracies in nine lines than one would have supposed possible.

"The Fair of Sorochintsy." 221

scenario, filling the gaps with music of his own, Cherepnin has made hay of the scenario but used no music other than Mussorgsky's own, though to do so he has been obliged not only to fill out mere sketches (including scraps of Ukrainian folk-songs,* probably given Mussorgsky by Petrov) and to transfer completed numbers from one act to another, but even to borrow material from Mussorgsky's other works. Cherepnin himself has explained his method of filling the gaps in a foreword:

"I have drawn on the existing music of the opera, modifying and developing the material. In some cases, I have drawn on other compositions by Mussorgsky, using musical material corresponding in character and feeling to the given dramatic situation. In the orchestration I have followed the style of the composers of the Russian nationalist school as practised at the period when Mussorgsky composed this opera."

Thus, for instance, one of the themes of the duets between Parasya and Gritsko—pp. 62 and 178 of the Bessel vocal score—at the end of Acts I and III is taken from the song, "On the Don"; on the other hand it is difficult to detect any connection between

---

* Ukrainian folk-music betrays Polish and other "western" influences. See, for instance, the not very interesting melody associated with Cherevik (pages 25, 44, etc., of the Bessel vocal score), a tune also used by Rimsky-Korsakov in Act II of "Christmas Eve," another Gogol opera.

the tranquil "Child's Song" of 1868 and the joyous outburst of the lovers at the end of Act III (bottom of p. 174 *et seq.*) for which it is employed. But perhaps the lovers are supposed to be thinking of the future.

It must be admitted that on the whole Cherepnin has succeeded admirably. But it seems a pity that he should have found it necessary to shift the *hopak*, intended for the end of Act I, to the end of the opera, and to transfer Gritsko's *dumka* from Act III to Act I. (Incidentally, the lovely theme of the *dumka* will be familiar to everyone from its appearance towards the end of the Rimsky-Korsakov version of "Night on the Bare Mountain"; the explanation is that Mussorgsky had thought of introducing the "Night" as a dream—or rather nightmare—intermezzo between Acts I and II of "The Fair.") Still, the greater part of the opera remains as Mussorgsky roughed it out, and there has been very little "editing" on the lines of Rimsky-Korsakov's revision of "Boris."

In the introduction, "A Hot Day in Little Russia," inspired by Gogol's opening paragraph, one of the loveliest prose passages in Russian literature, Mussorgsky's intentions indicated in the orchestral sketches, are carried out more faithfully than in the better-known Lyadov version. The first part of Act I (pp. 6-36 of the vocal score)—the fair chorus, adapted from that in "Mlada," Parasya's little solo and her father's phrase, the gypsy's tale, the trio,

"The Fair of Sorochintsy." 223

Cherevik's brush with his would-be son-in-law, and the reprise of the fair-music—was all completed in vocal score by Mussorgsky. And the comic scene, mainly based on two folk-songs between Cherevik and his crony, was also written by Mussorgsky and almost certainly intended for this part of the work. With the appearance of Khivrya the hand of the adapter takes the pen. As already mentioned, Gritsko's *dumka* was taken bodily from its place in Act III and inserted here; the rest of the act is an ingenious pastiche. One composition heavily drawn on here by Cherepnin is Salammbô's prayer, from the opera abandoned by Mussorgsky in 1866; Parasya's *poco meno tranquillo* passage (p. 59), the *andantino molto sostenûto* (p. 67), and the end of the duet (already resuscitated in "Boris") on p. 70 —all come from this prayer. So does the *poco sostenuto* (p. 176) in Act III.

The greater part of Act II (pp. 72-140 of the Bessel score) is also Mussorgsky's own; and Cherepnin has skilfully drawn on the "Bare Mountain" music among other things for the final scene. Act III is a different matter. Finding no material available—except Gritsko's *dumka*, already used elsewhere—Cherepnin has frankly abandoned the first part of the act as planned by Mussorgsky and begun with Parasya's beautiful song, a number occasionally heard on the concert platform. Except this song and the final *hopak*, this short act is entirely pastiche.

Mussorgsky's music contains some lovely pages and some broadly humorous ones (e.g., the Cherevik-crony scene in Act I, and the scene between Khivrya and her lover in Act II), but the falling off of his inspiration in this opera is unmistakable. During this last phase of his life he was much preoccupied by "a sort of melody shaped by human speech, the incorporation of recitative in melody. . . . I should like to call it 'intelligently justified' melody." "The Fair of Sorochintsy" contains a good deal of this "intelligently justified" melody—and the result is not particularly impressive. But let us be fair. If "The Fair" were the work of a lesser man than the composer of "Boris Godunov," we should welcome its sheafs of pleasant tunes, its grotesque humour and its charming colour without grumbling that it is not more than it is. Even as it is, it is one of the best of all Russian comic operas.

XVIII.—"EUGENE ONEGIN" AND TCHAÏKOVSKY'S MARRIAGE.

The full story of Tchaïkovsky's extraordinary marriage and the whole truth about his abnormality have never yet been told. Probably they never will be, for the very few persons who might have enlightened us are no longer living and it is improbable that any fresh documents will be discovered. The composer's brother Modest, in his monumental "Life and Letters" (the English edition of which is very much abridged), deals with the episode very much as a brother might be expected to. As for the unhappy widow, who survived her nominal husband for many years, she was always mentally unbalanced and towards the end of her life had to be confined in a lunatic asylum. Her somewhat romantic reminiscences of her husband were published in 1931, but as far as I have been able to discover she never made any definite statement about the catastrophe, except that "Peter was in no way to blame." On the other hand, the fact that she was still alive sealed the lips of others and obliged Kashkin, for instance, to suppress the relevant part of his memoirs, one of the most important of all the first-hand documents concerning Tchaïkovsky's life. However, this suppressed part was published just after the Revolution with other Tchaïkovsky letters and documents, and, although Kashkin leaves several vital points untouched, he records an extremely interesting confession of the composer's, according to which his marriage was intimately connected with the composition of "Eugene Onegin," indeed actually influenced by it.

In the spring of 1877 Tchaïkovsky was busy with his fourth symphony, to be dedicated to his new friend and benefactress, Madame von Meck. But he was never happy without an opera-subject in hand, and since hearing "Carmen" in Paris he particularly wanted "one dealing with real human beings, not lay-figures." Then one day in May, at the singer Lavrovskaya's, "the conversation fell upon opera texts," he wrote to Modest.

"Suddenly Lavrovskaya said, 'What about "Eugene Onegin"?' The idea struck me as very curious and I said nothing. Later, however, lunching alone at a restaurant, I remembered 'Onegin,' . . . and found the idea by no means so absurd. . . . I soon made up my mind and set off at once in search of Pushkin's works. . . . I was delighted when I read the poem. I spent a sleepless night:

result—the scenario of a splendid opera on Pushkin's text. The very next day I went to Shilovsky, and he is now working like the wind at my scenario. . . . You can't imagine how keen I am on this subject, how glad I am to have got away from all the usual Pharaohs, Ethiopian princesses, poisonings and suchlike. What a wealth of poetry there is in 'Onegin'! I quite see that the opera will have too little action, too little stage-effect, but these defects are counterbalanced by the great poetic wealth, the truth to life and simplicity of the happenings, and the genius of Pushkin's verses."

We must now take up the story in the words of Tchaïkovsky's verbal account to Kashkin, given a good many years later:

"In April or the beginning of May, 1877, I received a rather long letter with a declaration of love; the letter was signed A. Milyukova, and the writer stated that her love had originated several years before when she had been a pupil at the Conservatoire."

(He then went on to explain that he had no recollection of any Miss Milyukova, a piano pupil of Langer's.)

"At this very time I was exclusively occupied by the thought of 'Eugene Onegin,' i.e., of Tatyana, whose letter above all attracted me to this composition. Having no libretto as yet, but only a sort of general plan of the opera, I began to write the music of the letter scene, submitting to an irresistible inward urge to undertake this particular work, in the excitement of which I not only forgot about Miss Milyukova but even lost her letter, or hid it so well that I couldn't find it, and remembered about it only some time later when I received a second letter. Completely engrossed in the composition, I had so familiarised myself with the figure of Tatyana that she had become for me a living person in living surroundings. I loved Tatyana and was terribly indignant with Onegin, who seemed to me a cold, heartless coxcomb. On receiving Miss Milyukova's second letter, I was ashamed of myself and even felt indignant with myself for my attitude to her. In this second letter she complained bitterly of not having received a reply, adding that if the second letter shared the same fate as the first, there would be nothing left for her but to put an end to herself. In my mind all this became identified with the idea of Tatyana [who likewise takes the initiative in writing to the man she loves]; I myself, it seemed to me, had behaved incomparably worse than Onegin, and I was sincerely angry with myself for my heartless attitude to this girl who was in love with me. As in this second letter Miss Milyukova enclosed her address, I went there at once—and so our acquaintanceship began. . . . At this first meeting I told her that I could not reciprocate her love, but that she aroused my sincere sympathy. She replied that my sympathy was dear to her and that she could be satisfied with it—or words to that effect. I promised to see her frequently and I kept my word. . . . In my mind there was constantly that feeling of indignation at Onegin's careless, thoughtless attitude to Tatyana. To behave like Onegin [i.e., to tell her coldly and politely that he did not love her] seemed to me heartless and simply not to be thought of on my part. I was in a sort of delirium. All the time concentrating my thoughts on the opera, I was almost unconscious of everything else."

Yet he was conscious of one thing: that it would never do for any of his colleagues at the Conservatoire to know of the affair.

"I was persuaded that if any of you learned of it, then all would have to be finished and it would be impossible for me to act as I wanted to. I certainly couldn't have given myself any reason for this belief, but nevertheless there it was. All this confused shilly-shallying did not particularly agitate or disquieten me, but it hindered my composing and I decided to get the matter settled finally so as to be free of it."

And in that extraordinary state of mind Tchaïkovsky says he went to the girl, told her again that he could never love her—but that, if she still wanted to marry him he would be her husband! She agreed and the wedding was fixed for the near future, though Antonina was sworn to secrecy, "otherwise the wedding could not take place." He still feared, above all, that his colleagues would intervene.

"Having made this decision, I was perfectly unconscious of its importance and did not even consider what it would mean to me; it was indispensable to remove as soon as possible everything that prevented my concentration on the idea of the opera which possessed my whole being, and it seemed to me most simple and natural to act in this way. Then, having entrusted all the trouble and preparation of the wedding to Antonina, I felt as if I had rid myself of a burden and went away to the country, to Shilovsky's, who was working at the libretto of 'Eugene Onegin,' and spent the best part of a month [practically the whole of June] with him, working all the time and feeling perfectly satisfied and happy, since no one hindered me, and Shilovsky worked at the libretto with such enthusiasm that his cheerfulness infected me."

Shilovsky was a wealthy man. His estate of Glebovo was very fine, with exceptionally beautiful surroundings, and Tchaïkovsky worked away in a sort of blissful dream.

"As for the new way of life I was about to begin, I hardly remembered it at all, and only somewhere deep within me stirred an uneasy expectation of something I didn't want to think about, considering it useless to do so—and still more, disturbing."

But a letter from Antonina recalled him to the unpleasant reality. On June 23 (July 5), with two-

Tchaïkovsky's Marriage.   231

thirds of his opera sketched out, he broke the news of his impending marriage to his family, but even when he left Glebovo he lied to Shilovsky, pretending that his aged father had sent for him to go to Petersburg. On July 6 (18) he was married in Moscow.

After a week or two of married life, when Tchaïkovsky for the first time realised the full horror of his position, there was a temporary separation. Under the pretext of going to the Caucasus to take a mineral water cure, the bridegroom fled to his sister's home, where he completed the piano score of "Onegin" and began to orchestrate it and also scored the first movement of the F minor Symphony. In September he rejoined his wife in Moscow and spent a fortnight there in a state bordering on insanity. An attempt to commit suicide "in a natural looking way" (by catching pneumonia in the ice-cold river) having failed, he induced his brother Anatol to send him a faked telegram in the name of the St. Petersburg conductor, Napravnik, and fled to the northern capital on September 24 (October 6). Anatol, who met him at the station, hardly recognised him, "his face had so changed in the course of a month." After a terrible nerve storm, he lay unconscious for nearly forty-eight hours. The doctor ordered that there should be no attempt to resume married life, that if possible he should never even see his wife again. Anatol took his brother abroad at once. Both the symphony and "Onegin" were completed during that winter of convalescence at Clarens and in Venice.

This romantic story of the influence of the "Onegin" letter scene on the composer's own life is so fantastic as to demand a few words of comment. On the one hand, Tchaïkovsky (as we see from this narrative alone, to say nothing of a dozen other confessions in his letters) never hesitated to lie when it suited his purpose and never seems to have felt the least shame about it afterwards. Living in his own neurotic dream-world, he appears to have had very little moral sense where truth was concerned—probably often being only semi-conscious of what the truth really was. May he not have been romancing a little to Kashkin, especially as this account is not reconcilable in every detail with that which emerges from his letters of the same period? On the other hand, Kashkin (whose own veracity is beyond question) says that, knowing Tchaïkovsky intimately, he finds it perfectly easy to understand how he thought and acted as he did, irresponsibly, as if living in a dream.

Finally, I should like to draw attention to a curious point in the music of "Onegin." As we have seen, the first part of the opera to be written, the part which dominated all the rest in the composer's mind, was the famous letter aria. Towards the end of this, as Tatyana's emotion reaches its height, a horn phrase of melting warmth is heard:

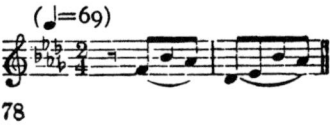

answering a descending oboe passage. That phrase, or rather its first few notes, curiously interpenetrates nearly the whole of the music of the opera. It is a sort of motto theme for the work, though no doubt an unconscious one. (To have used it deliberately as it is used would have been pointless.) We hear it first in the duet behind the scenes which opens the first act. It occurs in a little phrase piped out by flute and oboe at the end of the quartet when Onegin first looks at the shy girl "rather familiarly" and then goes up to her. We hear it again in the viola phrases which close the love scene between Olga and Lensky, and once more (in the orchestra) near the beginning of the second scene, when Tatyana says to her old nurse: "Amuse me; and tell me some tale of long ago." In the letter scene itself it occurs quite early, in a different musical context. It assumes two different forms in Gremin's aria in Act III, and it occurs again in Tatyana's sweeping phrase which dominates the last passionate scene of the opera. It is an interesting case of a little temporary melodic obsession.

XIX.—GLAZUNOV: THE END OF AN EPISODE.

"Glazunov," said his first biographer, Ossovsky, "has effected a reconciliation between the Russian music of his time and western music. In this he has played an even more decisive part than Tchaïkovsky, who was in the thick of the struggle between the two tendencies and therefore psychologically incapacitated from playing the part of peacemaker." Ossovsky was writing nearly thirty years ago, and this judgment of his has been often quoted and not infrequently disputed. But, except that it seems to attribute to Glazunov an active individual rôle in the reconciliation, it does neatly summarise his historical position. He did "reconcile" Russian nationalism with the main currents of western music in his own compositions, though the reconciliation was a rather lamb-and-wolf-like affair. But in that he was not unique. Arensky and a host of minor composers did the same. Glazunov was only the most important figure of that generation, a generation of epigones.

Glazunov.

When on March 17—29, 1882, the not yet seventeen-year-old Glazunov made his début with his first symphony—"young in inspiration but already mature in technique and structure," as Rimsky-Korsakov said—it would have been natural to prophesy that he would ripen into the finest fruit of all the Russian school, a Brahms to Borodin's Schumann and Korsakov's Mendelssohn. But although this school then appeared to be at its most flourishing, its decline had already begun, and it fell to Glazunov to lead its comfortable, self-satisfied slide into ignominious mediocrity. The force of the great artistic, intellectual and political waves that had swept Russia in the sixties had been spent even before 1882. The great literary age was over; political reaction had set in. In music it was the same. The "mighty handful" had broken up. Balakirev had written only one thing in ten years. Mussorgsky was dead and even his genius, physically undermined, had deteriorated in his last years. Borodin had done practically all his best work; he, too, showed a strange weakening of creative power in the eighties. As for Rimsky-Korsakov, he had been the first to desert to the academics. As a composer he was almost completely sterile throughout the eighties; then (with Glazunov) he came under the influence of Wagner and kept turning aside to write distressing quantities of lifeless, colourless music in vain attempts to escape the limitations of narrow nationalism.

This was the environment into which Glazunov was musically "born." He and Rimsky-Korsakov's other pupils were taught to admire only the superficial characteristics of the earlier nationalist movement. The use of folk-songs, a folk-songish flavour in one's own melodies, brilliant, colourful orchestration—these were good. But "clumsiness," "eccentricity," "amateurishness"—terms of abuse for the very qualities that now interest us most in the work of the "mighty handful"—these were condemned. The first movement of Borodin's E flat Symphony was something entirely new in symphonic construction, yet Korsakov—himself completely lacking in the symphonic sense—seems never to have set it as a model to his students. Apart from orchestration, he taught just what the professors of every conservatoire in Germany, France or England taught: the technique of composition employed by the German classical and romantic masters. Thus Glazunov learned to speak music with a Russian accent, but not to think musically in Russian. (And even the accent had almost worn off by the time he was thirty.) Besides, Tchaïkovsky was the most popular composer in Russia during the eighties and Glazunov was not slow in succumbing to his influence. Personal friendship also tightened this particular bond. Incidentally, both composers are reputed to have been heavy drinkers, and the whole of this circle—Glazunov, Tchaïkovsky, Arensky, Lyadov and the publisher Belaiev—scandalised Korsakov by their all-night sittings in restaurants. Belaiev was particularly closely connected with Glazunov's fortunes. The whole history of his famous publishing house is bound up with Glazunov's creative career.

We must look back again for a moment to the brilliant opening of that career. About 1878 or 1879 Mme. Glazunova, an amateur pianist, wife of a wealthy St. Petersburg book publisher, began to take elementary theory lessons from Rimsky-Korsakov. Balakirev, who had made the introduction, was also interested in her fourteen-year-old son's attempts at composition, and on December 23, 1879 (January 4, 1880, N.S.), the boy "Sasha" came to Korsakov for his first harmony lesson. The lessons continued once a week on Sundays, and his master tells us that "his musical development progressed not by days but by hours. From the very beginning of the lessons my relationship with Sasha began to change little by little from that of master and pupil to one of friendship, despite the difference in our years. Balakirev also took a considerable part in Sasha's development, playing a great deal to him and talking to him."

Fifteen months later, Balakirev conducted the famous first performance of his "little Glinka's" first symphony. "It had a great success," says Korsakov. "The public were astounded when the composer came forward in his high school uniform to acknowledge their applause. But there were a few snarls from the critics. And there were caricatures depicting Glazunov as a child at the breast. Rumour asserted that the symphony had not been written by him but commissioned by his wealthy parents from you know whom'—and other things in the same vein." Four or five months after, Korsakov included his pupil's symphony in one of his programmes at the Moscow Exhibition. "Before the first rehearsal of the symphony," he writes, "a tall, handsome man came up to me, introduced himself as Mitrofan Petrovich Belaiev, and asked permission to attend all the rehearsals. He had been so completely enraptured by Glazunov's symphony at its first performance that he had come to Moscow specially to hear it again. Belaiev, extremely wealthy, went so far in his enthusiasm as to have the symphony printed at his own expense by Röder, of Leipzig, and in March, 1884, wishing to hear it again and to hear Glazunov's new "Characteristic Suite," Op. 9, he hired the Opera orchestra and the hall of the Petropavlovsky College and held a private rehearsal for the benefit of a few friends.

The one action led to the foundation of the famous publishing business, the other to the institution of the Russian Symphony Concerts, in both of which undertakings Glazunov soon held important (and later, controlling) positions. Add to this the fact that in 1906 he became director of the St. Petersburg Conservatoire, and it will be seen that during the decade before the war Glazunov was practically the musical dictator of Russia, challenged only latterly by Kussevitsky. Abroad he was from the first unquestioningly accepted as one of the most important Russian composers. Even the Revolution did not unseat him from the directorship of the Conservatoire, though it clipped his wings in other directions. In spite of various difficulties, he remained in Russia till 1926, when he retired to Paris.

Glazunov's creative career contrasts rather pitifully with this record of worldly success. It is more or less epitomised by the statement of one significant fact: that he wrote eight symphonies before he was forty and lived to be seventy-one without writing a ninth. Almost the only important work he composed after 1904 was the not very interesting piano Concerto in F minor (finished in 1911). At first he wrote prolifically and facilely, and it seems that he wrote himself out. That, of course, had nothing to do with the historical background that partially conditioned the nature of his music. The weakness lay in himself, not in anything external. He certainly did some of his most attractive work in his early days while he was still "playing the sedulous ape" to the older nationalists—e.g., the symphonic poem, "Stenka Razin," Op. 13 (written in 1885) and the Slavonic Quartet, Op. 26. But if he had merely gone on producing good imitations of Borodin and Korsakov he must have petered out even more quickly than he did. His own natural gift was for fluent, pleasant, not very distinguished melody; for twenty years it flowed from him in a stream, and when he poured it into the suitable mould of the ballet he was able to cast delightful forms: "Raymonda," "Ruses d'Amour," "The Seasons," the orchestral "Valses de Concert."

When he chose the symphonic mould he was less successful. A Glazunov symphony is just an uninterrupted flow of melodious ideas, laid out according to the classical or neo-romantic (Lisztian) forms, lusciously harmonised and beautifully orchestrated. But nothing ever happens to these ideas. The flow of music never gets anywhere. Climaxes are ar-arranged; the current rises and falls; there are delightful touches of orchestration (such as the deliciously sugary trio of the fourth symphony) and endless—and effortless—technical skill. Melodious phrases are beautifully interwoven, ingeniously transformed. But there is no growth, not even a sense of direction.

Moreover, practically every one of Glazunov's symphonies sounds like the others. He probably put his best work into the fourth, fifth and sixth (1894-1896), yet each of these leaves more or less the same general impression; you distinguish them in memory only by external things, because No. 6 has a set of pretty variations, and so on.

Take the chief subjects of the first movements of Glazunov's fourth, fifth, sixth and eighth symphonies. There is no concealed identity in these suave, rather feminine themes, though they have certain obvious traits in common. But the almost-identity of key is symptomatic. They are different, but each is just a little too like the others to give a distinctive cachet to the movement it dominates. Glazunov himself must have been conscious that he was, in effect, writing the same symphony over and over again when he stopped writing it in 1904. That combination of lyrical spontaneity and polished craftsmanship should have produced a first-rate miniaturist, but Glazunov did very little in the smaller forms. His short piano pieces are as negligible as his incidental music for the stage (to Wilde's "Salome" and a Passion play, "The King of the Jews"), and he wrote hardly any songs. But in the variation form—the chain of miniatures—he did at least three charming pieces of work: the variations in the Quartet Suite, Op. 35, those in the Sixth Symphony, and the Theme and Variations for piano, Op. 72.

To sum up: Glazunov was a master of the craft of composition, gifted with genuine though limited creative talent. He produced a great quantity of music that is always pleasant to listen to—too consistently "pleasant"—and still more pleasant to play. (It was an axiom of his that good orchestral music should "play itself.") But as a youth he had promised so much more. The rose-strewn career of Balakirev's "little Glinka," wealthy *enfant gâté* of Russian music, with its record of uninterrupted outward success, remains after all a tragedy of brilliant promise only half fulfilled.

XX.—SOME PSYCHOLOGICAL PECULIARITIES OF RUSSIAN CREATIVE ARTISTS.

I must ask pardon for prefacing these observations with a piece of man-in-the-streetish logic: "All Russians are slightly mad. All painters, poets and musicians are slightly mad. Therefore, all Russian painters, poets and musicians are more than slightly mad." For there is just enough truth in that to make it worth thinking about. The psychological make-up of any creative artist is not only likely to be more unusual and more puzzling than that of the "average, sensual man" —that is, more interesting for its own sake—but is valuable for any light it may throw on his work And when the problem is complicated through the subject belonging to a nation with more marked psychological peculiarities than any other in Europe, it becomes extraordinarily fascinating. For while the specifically Latin or Teutonic or Keltic peculiarities can be distinguished and grouped and related to each other, those of the Slavs are inexplicable even (I think) to themselves, unconnected and, as we say for want of a better word, illogical. We can understand the Russian "tendency to pity," Russian pessimism, Russian optimism, and that peculiarly Russian form of laziness which Goncharov satirised in his "Oblomov," thereby giving a new word to the Russian language. These are only universal traits seen in the distorting mirror of a peculiar national temperament. But this temperament also produces phenomena which cannot be explained by anything in our own experience or that of other Western peoples. And I suggest that since these phenomena are not uncommon or noticeable only in minor artists, but occur frequently in the cases of writers and musicians of the first rank, they are worth comparing and studying simply as phenomena even if we cannot venture here to probe very deeply into their origins.

By far the most extraordinary of these phenomena is the tendency to stop and change direction in mid-career. The case most familiar to the average English reader is probably Tolstoy's. But his, if the most famous, is by no means the most remarkable. These crises vary, of course, in intensity. In their most violent forms the artist abandons his work altogether; with colder, less spiritual natures, for instance, Rimsky-Korsakov, the crisis causes only a temporary cessation of work and a radical change of style in the work itself. The crisis is

Some Psychological Peculiarities. 245

usually marked by dislike for the artist's own previous productions—a different matter from the passing self-doubts that afflict most artists from time to time—and there is usually a resumption of activity on the old lines after a more or less prolonged period of wandering in the wilderness.

The most tragic of all these cases is that of Gogol, for death overtook him at a time when his artistic convalescence may have been just beginning. Gogol's collapse after the single decade of activity (1831-42) into which he crowded practically the whole of his life-work is usually attributed to his religious mania, but there is quite as much evidence for the assumption that the religious mania was the result of this early and inexplicable decay of his creative faculty. (He was still in his early thirties.) We may put it that both were equally symptoms of the same mysterious malady of the spirit. At any rate, it is clear from Gogol's correspondence that his religious preoccupation was not a spontaneous passion, but an impotent longing to experience such a passion—of which he was completely incapable. He began to apologise for his masterpieces, writing in 1846 an epilogue to his "Revizor" of ten years earlier, in which that delightful comedy is "explained" as a piece of ethical symbolism. In 1848 he again began to interest himself in artistic matters, particularly in the folk-songs and ballads which were his original literary roots, and worked at the second part of "Dead Souls," producing writing which seems to have delighted everyone to whom he read it. But a year or so later he had to write to Zhukovsky that he was overcome by "old age or temporary paralysis of my powers. . . . I do my best not to waste a minute . . . but work drags." Then, early in 1852, the death of a near friend seems to have induced a sudden intensification of his hypochondria; in a fit of religio-maniacal frenzy he burned all but a few fragments of the manuscript second part of "Deal Souls"—and died ten days later.

Many features of this case naturally remind one of Tolstoy's, but there is an even closer parallel in that of Balakirev. Here again we find an intensely egotistic, domineering personality, almost feverishly active during his twenties and early thirties—active not only as composer but as conductor, pianist, teacher and concert-entrepreneur; and again a rapid collapse of the creative faculty, accompanied by a mania, superstitious rather than genuinely religious. As early as 1861, ten years before the crisis, Balakirev had written to Stassov: "Very strange wishes arise in me; you would call them wild. I should like to burn all my compositions before I die. It is not worth while that people should be amused by my compositions." (Though, fortunately, he never carried out this intention as Gogol did on more than one occasion.) In other respects Gogol's and Balakirev's symptoms were remarkably similar. Both avoided society, even that

Some Psychological Peculiarities. 247

of their friends. Both concealed beneath an outward display of ultra-orthodoxy, an almost incredibly atavistic superstitiousness. Gogol actually confesses to "superstition" in his more intimate letters, and seems to have been terrified by thoughts and visions of the devil. And the originally suppressed passages of Rimsky-Korsakov's memoirs, only recently published, reveal that in the early 'seventies Balakirev began to pay mysterious visits to a "witch" who professed to divine the success of his undertakings, the designs of his enemies in the Petersburg musical world, and so on. It is significant that Rimsky-Korsakov thought his friend "believed not in God, but in the devil." But Balakirev weathered his spiritual storm with more success than Gogol. After a curious hegira of three years, spent as a minor official on the Warsaw railway, he gradually drifted back into the musical world, and later, after a quarter of a century's silence, even began to compose again with unweakened powers, the last decade of his life being remarkably productive.

The case of Tolstoy is too well known to call for much comment; its special interest lies in its enlightening differences. Tolstoy was one of the least neurotic of Russian artists; he enjoyed exceptional physical health and his intellect was far more positive and vigorous than Gogol's, for instance. Gogol was a great artist, but no thinker. So we find that *his* crisis is predominantly intellectual in character. Like Gogol, he condemns his own masterpieces on the ground that they are shallow and therefore "immoral." But the conviction which compels him to condemn them works through his conscious mind, along a path of relentless logic, instead of through the depths of the subconsciousness as with Gogol. Here again there was a resumption of genuine artistic creation after an interval of ten years (1876-1886), in "The Death of Ivan Ilyich," "The Kreutzer Sonata," and other works. Even Tolstoy's religious ideas were essentially intellectual. Spiritually, he was probably in precisely the same position as Gogol and Balakirev; that is, he was possessed by a very strong will-to-religion, but had very little genuine religiosity.

Still more enlightening is the case of Rimsky-Korsakov, who never pretended to be anything but a rationalist all his life, though some of his operas betray an inclination to pantheistic ideology. Rimsky-Korsakov was one of the most intellectual of Russian musicians—sane, temperamentally rather cold, and, for a Russian, curiously unspiritual. The account of his case is therefore of special interest for, considering its general parallelism with the others discussed here, it casts doubt on any theory that these psycho-physical disturbances in the careers of Russian artists are religious *in origin* and suggests that the religious symptoms are only results produced by the disturbances in certain natures. In a man constituted like Rimsky-Korsakov the crisis, as one would expect, took a less serious form. The first signs of trouble (he tells us in his very precisely and objectively written memoirs) occurred in the summer of 1892, when he was about forty-eight. The symptoms were weariness and a distaste for musical work, coupled with a desire to embark on voluminous philosophical dissertations (cf. Gogol's didactic "Correspondence with my Friends" and Tolstoy's numerous tracts in the period following the publication of "Anna Karenina"). In Korsakov's case "the persistent thought of writing a self-criticism" suggested a book on Russian music; but this in turn led him into the wider field of musical æsthetics and history; and thence through æsthetics in general to philosophy—a sudden feverish and unnatural desire to get to the bottom of all things. All his studies seem to have been wild and unsystematic, betraying a serious slackening of mental discipline. "For whole days long I pondered over these matters, turning my own disconnected ideas hither and thither. Then one morning, at the end of August or in September, I felt great fatigue, in conjunction with a violent rush of blood to the head and complete confusion of all my thoughts." Alarmed, he gave up his reading and spent much time in the open air. "Directly I was alone my thoughts persecuted me like delusive phantoms. I also pondered over religion and meditated a humble reconciliation with Balakirev."

After a time he seemed to have recovered. "But my love for music had cooled off and I thought of nothing but my philosophical education." He read Spinoza and Herbert Spencer, and various æsthetic writings and histories of philosophy, buying new books nearly every day ("dashing from one to the other"), making marginal notes, and so on. Again he set to work on a book on musical æsthetics, and again this led him into the wilderness of metaphysics in general—and brought on a renewal of the old physical symptoms, "with giddiness and a sense of weight and pressure. I suffered greatly from these phenomena, which were also generally attended by certain tyrannnising ideas." The production of "Mlada" in October, 1892, brought distraction but did not revive the composer's impulse to create. A whole year elapsed before he even touched a piano seriously and felt for a few days "in a musical frame of mind." He began to think of writing musical text-books, and again these grew into "philosophical dissertations." Not till the spring of 1894 did Rimsky-Korsakov feel any impulse to compose again; then for about a year he produced some of his best work. But in the middle of his work on "Sadko" he was quite suddenly overwhelmed by "unbearable weariness and indifference . . . even disgust for work," though this condition, he adds, had nothing in common with his previous experience. "Sadko," one of his best and most characteristic works, was suddenly followed by a complete change and serious deterioration in Korsakov's musical style. Only in "Saltan" and in his

Some Psychological Peculiarities. 251

last two operas, "Kitezh" and "The Golden Cockerel," did he return to the manner and qualitative level of his earlier music. And by way of footnote to Rimsky-Korsakov's case, we must observe that his pupil Stravinsky has changed *his* musical style just as completely and suddenly in mid-career, though we naturally know nothing as yet of Stravinsky's *inner* life.

In addition, there are certain peculiarities of the Russian mind which seem to affect Russian creative art more directly, peculiarities of artistic technique rather than of artistic temperament. One is a very strong tendency to repetition with or without slight differences, instead of development of a subject, both in a single work and in a series of works. Everyone will be able to think of constantly recurrent types and ideas in the novels of Tolstoy and Dostoevsky. We can see the same trait in Mussorgsky's and Rimsky-Korsakov's tendency to modify, instead of genuinely developing, their musical material in any single work, as well as in the latter's constant harking back to similar musical ideas and dramatic situations in one opera after another. Borodin's persistent hammering away at his chief theme in the first movement of his B minor Symphony and Tolstoy's driving home of his theory of history toward the end of "War and Peace" betray precisely the same cast of mind working in totally different mediums. Again: Russian composers and novelists alike are generally weak *archi-*

tecturally. Their wholes consist of separate, intensely felt episodes, brilliantly juxtaposed rather than organically growing from each other. A hundred years ago the critic Chaadaev pointed out in his "Letters on the Philosophy of History" (Moscow: 1836) that "there is a profound lacuna in our intellectual organisation. The capacity for logical thinking, the spirit of method, and the feeling for continuity, are entirely lacking in us."

One trait, above all, marks out the typical Russian creative artist from those of other nations—his relationship to his subject-matter, to whatever inspires him. The most superficial student of Russian literature knows that its predominant note is realism: the tendency, that is, to start from a basis of given facts and, broadly speaking, to portray them closely and accurately. The artistic faculty is employed in the selection and vivid presentation of the facts rather than in imaginative invention. And we find among Russian musicians the same need of a "given fact" as a nucleus for creative activity. In the musician's case this *donnée* may be either musical or extra-musical—a subjective emotion, a poem, a visual impression. It may be straining the point to adduce Tchaïkovsky's immediate expression of "raw" emotion, in his last two symphonies, in contrast with the Western musical tradition of mediate, sublimated expression. But there can be no question of the innate realism of opera-reformers like Dargomïzhsky and Mussorgsky.

Some Psychological Peculiarities. 253

Even Rimsky-Korsakov turned in this direction at times. "I want the note to be the direct expression of the word," said Dargomïzhsky. And Mussorgsky again and again stated his aims in almost precisely the same words. Their musical ideal, which had next to nothing in common with Wagner's, was a sort of literal translation of words and even gestures into tones, a type of music very "close" to its verbal or pantomimic *donnée*.

But the predominantly lyrical, non-dramatic type of Russian composer seems in equal need of some "given" basis; it must be a purely musical one—and he finds it in folk-song. We see Glinka, Balakirev, Mussorgsky in his lyrical moods, Rimsky-Korsakov and the rest continually borrowing from and imitating and leaning on folk-song, not by way of relaxation or patriotic gesture or simple, unconscious instinct as Western composers have always done, but as the very foundation of their art—and not getting very far away from folk-music without seriously weakening the quality of their production. They cannot *invent* with much success, but given an "external" subject they can work miracles. In this respect also there is a curious parallelism between Gogol and Balakirev, perhaps partly due to the fact that neither was a Great Russian. Gogol was a Ukrainian, of Cossack stock, and Balakirev had Tatar blood. At any rate, both showed a strong penchant for the romantic and heroic; and both, dependent on "given" subjects, worked on these foundations with extraordinary exuberance. The realistic basis of "Dead Souls" is obvious; but it is not so well known that the themes of Gogol's early fantastic stories are all borrowed from folk-lore, and are marvellously modified and decorated by his artistic imagination. As Janko Lavrin has put it, "his imagination is not inventive at all but intensifying." Is not that largely true of Dostoevsky as well? And that phrase also exactly defines the nature of Balakirev's musical imagination. He seldom invented themes of his own; his admitted borrowings are wholesale; but his creative fancy so decorated and intensified the most insignificant scraps of borrowed folk-music that his compositions are as completely the products of his own unique mind as the "Evenings on a Farm near Dikanka" are entirely Gogolian. Whereas Gogol and Balakirev, the most romantic of Russian prose-writers and composers respectively, thus embroidered and intensified their themes, the predominant Russian tendency has been toward classic, apparently objective treatment of data. But the existence of fundamental data seems to be equally necessary in all cases. To say that is not to disparage the Russian creative faculty, but to help to define its peculiar nature. It is no doubt true that all art depends to some extent on such data, but none so closely and obviously as that of the Russians.

XXI.—THE EVOLUTION OF RUSSIAN HARMONY.

Can one speak of specifically Russian harmony, as distinct from German, Italian or French harmony? It would be rash to assert that national characteristics are as evident in the harmony of a people's music as in the melodic outline or the rhythm, though it is undeniably true that the harmony of Bellini and Donizetti is simpler and more limpid than that of Spohr and Marschner, Verdi's than Wagner's, or Puccini's than Strauss's. But Russian art-music grew up in peculiar conditions, partially isolated from contemporary Western music, mainly in the hands of composers who were (for good or ill) amateurs, closely linked with a folk-music marked by various tonal peculiarities. The first important composer saturated with the processes of "school" harmony—Tchaïkovsky—did not appear till the late 1860's; Rimsky-Korsakov knew practically nothing of text-book harmony till the middle of the 1870's. The chromatic harmony of Chopin and Liszt exercised little influence on Russian music till towards the end of the '60's and another twenty years passed before the influence of the mature Wagnerian style made itself felt. Apart altogether from the fact that Russian musicians have always shown a peculiar intellectual interest in what we may call the curiosities of harmony and that two or three of them have been revolutionary innovators, it is hardly surprising that the harmonic style of the Russian school in general, and of the "mighty handful" in particular, bears an unmistakable stamp of what we may as well call "nationality."

Had they only known it, these admirers of "the people" and of popular music might have borrowed from the people and adapted for their own ends even a rudimentary system of harmony. But the researches of Melgunov into the polyphonic nature of Russian folk-music were not made public till 1879, too late to exercise any influence on the development of Russian art-music. Glinka and the "mighty handful" were acquainted with folk melody only. When Rimsky-Korsakov talks in his memoirs about the difficulty of harmonising his two collections of folk-songs "in a simple, truly Russian manner," he means not "in the peasant manner," of which he was then ignorant, and which he thought "barbarous" when he did learn about it, but "in the harmonic tradition of Glinka." For "Russian harmony," apart from the audacities of

Dargomïzhsky and Mussorgsky, who evidently experimented at the piano empirically, was mainly evolved from the practice of Glinka.

Now Glinka's harmonic language was derived (a) from intimate knowledge of the scores of Mozart, Cherubini, Méhul, Beethoven, Bellini and Donizetti, (b) from two brief periods of study of harmony and counterpoint with J. L. Fuchs and Francesco Basili, and some four or five months of more serious work under Siegfried Dehn. He had. therefore, at least a better equipment than the Alyabievs and Varlamovs and other dilettanti who had half-baked their music from a pitifully limited range of chords. There are plenty of traces of dilettantism in Glinka, too—for instance, a pronounced tendency to "sit on" a note, either as a pedal or as a harmonic pivot—but his love of Beethoven taught him the power of genuine harmonic movement, while the Italians, though they did not help him to escape from a limited convention, strongly impressed him with the virtues of simple and limpid harmony.

The tendency to build chords all round a harmonic pivot or to sustain pedal-points—often very short—in one part or another may have originated in feeble meanderings at the piano, but later developed into a very characteristic feature of Glinka's style and produced some very striking results. An outstanding example is the E flat in the scene of Lyudmila's abduction in "Ruslan"; it appears as a unison at the end of a whole-tone scale passage and becomes by turns the third of a C flat major chord, the tonic of a minor triad, the seventh of a diminished seventh, the third of a C minor chord, the fifth of a dominant seventh on A flat, the third (enharmonically) of a dominant seventh on B natural, the root of a dominant seventh, and the root of a major triad; and it is finally sustained as a dominant pedal throughout the ensuing canon and chorus in A flat (forty-six bars in slow time). But the following example from "A Life for the Tsar" of a brief passing pedal-effect is more typical of Glinka's normal harmonic procedure:

(Notice the C sharp, which has the effect of a "foreign" note in a dominant seventh, instead of conveying a major ninth feeling; Glinka not infrequently uses such colourful "foreign" notes.)

Glinka often shows an affection for piquant chords (augmented and diminished triads) and intervals (seconds and sevenths). In conjunction with his love of pedals, this produces such effects as:

Evolution of Russian Harmony. 259

80

(a "magic" theme in "Ruslan"). In conjunction with the whole-tone scale, it produces Ex. 14, also a "magic" effect. Indeed these harmonies are generally associated with the magic or fantastic (see also Ex. 81b below). It will be noticed that Ex. 14 is not only based on the whole-tone scale but actually composed in the whole-tone mode. In the overture, however, a descending whole-tone scale is harmonised with alternate major triads and second inversions of diminished triads, producing an effect of rapid modulation rather than temporarily destroying the key-feeling altogether.

On the whole, of course, Glinka's harmony is essentially diatonic and respectful of contemporary conventions—in "A Life for the Tsar" often as conventional as that of his Italian models. He harmonises even a modal melody (e.g., the fine unison chorus with quasi-balalaïka accompaniment in Act I of "A Life for the Tsar," part of which is quoted in Ex. 7) diatonically. The chromatic chords he uses are for the most part drawn only from the common stock-in-trade of the day. The one really characteristic and recurrent chromaticism in Glinka's harmony is the sharpened fifth (or flattened sixth) of the scale.* This enharmonic identity of the leading note of the relative minor with the third of that favourite romantic chord, the minor triad on the subdominant (cf. the opening of the "Midsummer Night's Dream" overture and Schubert *passim*) gives it a peculiar strength—if "strong" is the word to apply to an effect of such voluptuous melancholy. Glinka is very fond of using it to produce brief cadential modulations to the relative minor, often so brief that one feels them to be less truly modulations than chromatic extensions of the major; but even its transient appearance as a passing-note is sufficient to cast a minor shadow over the music (see Ex. 8, for instance). And it is not perhaps altogether a coincidence that the same note, the sharpened fifth, hints at once at the augmented triad on the tonic. Such examples as Nos. 12 and 16b, and the two following, will be recognised immediately as typically Russian harmony:

---

* One seeks this in vain in the music of his most important Russian contemporary, Verstovsky.

(b) Ruslan.

(See also Ex. 80, where, as in 81 b, the key is B flat major, not G minor.)

The "Kamarinskaya" example also shows the flattened leading-note, characteristic of a good many Russian folk-songs. It would be straining a point to suggest that Glinka got the idea of the whole-tone scale from folk-music; it was obviously a purely intellectual conception. But it is feasible that some of these tonal peculiarities of Russian folk-tunes—the sharpened fourth of some and the flattened seventh of others—together with the sharpened fifth or flattened sixth noticed above, predisposed him and later Russian musicians to accept the whole-tone scale more readily than Western musicians. Once these notes were accepted as normal chromatic alterations and extensions of the major scale, it must have been easy to accept them in series for their own sakes.

The harmony of Balakirev and his circle in the early 1860's was essentially that of Glinka. Balakirev's own early works—the "Overture on Three Russian Themes," "Russia," the "King Lear" music, and so on—contain little, harmonically, that Glinka would not have written. But Balakirev's young disciples did not all possess his (and

Glinka's) technical knowledge or their instinctive feeling for clean part-writing. Rimsky-Korsakov, for instance, afterwards confessed to complete ignorance at this time of even the rudiments of harmony. He composed empirically at the piano, guided only by his ear and curbed only by Balakirev's blue pencil, and it is certain that if we could get hold of his early scores—the symphonic poem "Sadko," "Antar," "The Maid of Pskov" and the rest—in their original forms, instead of in the drastically revised versions in which we know them, we should find a good crop of amusing curiosities, possibly elementary blunders and ineptitudes, cheek by jowl with flashes of untrammelled genius, as in the case of Mussorgsky.

With Mussorgsky we know, for we now possess his compositions in their original forms. He, too, was an empiricist of genius—of far greater harmonic genius than Rimsky-Korsakov at any period of his life. Not only was Mussorgsky an empiricist; about 1868 he came strongly under the influence of Dargomïzhsky, who was not only a good deal of an empiricist but, as we have already seen, a daring harmonic experimenter. I have already, in Chapter IV, discussed Dargomïzhsky's three orchestral pieces, with their harmonic asperities and ingenuities, and drawn attention to the contrast between Dargomïzhsky's jejune "normal" harmonies and his bold experiments. In "The Stone

Guest," the work of his which exercised the strongest influence on Mussorgsky, this contrast is again very marked.

But Dargomïzhsky's experiments are of different kinds. There are the celebrated cases where, enlarging on a hint from Glinka, he explores the whole-tone mode. And there are such things as this, when Donna Anna reproaches Don Juan with being "a godless seducer, a devil incarnate":

which seems to be essentially a product of keyboard extemporising* and which Rimsky-Korsakov took it upon himself to "smooth out" when he prepared a new edition of the work in 1903. Broadly speaking, it is in the latter kind of harmonic experiment that Mussorgsky is most akin to Dargomïzhsky. It was from the older composer that he got the idea of finding expressive, purely empirical chords at the piano—chords and progressions justifiable solely on the ground of dramatic expression. His famous setting of the first act of Gogol's comedy, "The Marriage," is a perfect museum of these extraordinary (yet somehow curiously right)

---

* The fact that Ex. 82 can be accounted for theoretically does not affect the more important fact that Dargomïzhsky obviously arrived at it empirically.

conglomerations of notes, e.g., the progressions of consecutive minor seconds when Podkolesin walks across the room (end of the second scene and other places), or this:

where the first chord is explicable not by any theory of chord-structure but by the fact that it coincides with the first syllable of the word "skvernost" ("nastiness"). To this category, too, belong such passages in "Boris Godunov" as that which accompanies Shuisky's words, "I sought a chink and peered through watching him," in the Duma scene.

At the same time apparent empiricism is not always real empiricism. Sometimes when Mussorgsky appears to be arbitrarily doing something odd merely for the sake of oddness he is really obeying an instinct which many people—including Rimsky-Korsakov, as it appears—do not possess. Take this example from the innkeeper's song in "Boris":

Mussorgsky was not deliberately indulging here in false relation for its own sour sake. For the explanation of this passage and others like it we must remember that sharpened fifth (or flattened sixth) of which Glinka was so fond. The use of this particular chromatic effect is one of the commonest characteristics of nineteenth-century Russian harmony*; one finds it on page after page of any Russian "nationalist" score and on a good many of Tchaikovsky's—but almost always as a chromatic effect, a colourful decoration of the diatonic major scale.

Mussorgsky, on the other hand, obviously accepted both this note between the fifth and sixth degrees of the scale and the flattened form of the seventh as integral parts of the mode in which he was writing. In other words, he sometimes unconsciously thought in a nine-note scale. And if Glinka's chromaticism merely opened the way for that scale (see Ex. 81 a), the opening bars of "The Stone Guest" had gone a little farther along that way. In Rimsky-Korsakov's version of "Boris" Ex. 84 has naturally been "cleaned up"; the flattened seventh has disappeared altogether and we must be grateful to Korsakov for unaccountably leaving one A sharp—presumably reprieved on the ground that the bass is a quasi-ostinato figure:

---

* And, of course, not uncommon in plenty of non-Russian music (e.g., Wagner's "Good Friday" music).

Even that single A sharp is sufficient to give a suspicion of B minor to a passage really in D major. The tendency to confuse and mingle a major key with its relative minor is thoroughly typical of Russian harmony from Glinka onward (cf. Ex. 8 from "A Life for the Tsar") and made its way into Western music before the turn of the century. Dargomïzhsky in his "Fantasia on Finnish Themes" causes similar confusion between major and tonic minor by the very same tonal peculiarity as in Ex. 84—the use of an additional note (here written as a flattened sixth) between the fifth and sixth degrees of the major scale. For three bars a normal A major melody is given an ostinato bass on the notes A, F natural, E, F natural, D—apparently in A minor. From this to the actual telescoping of major and minor triads on the same root, as in the "Cercles mystérieux des adolescentes" of "The Rite of Spring," was a very small step indeed. Yet nearly half a century passed before Stravinsky took it.

Mussorgsky's modification and enlargement of the normal scales is by no means limited to the addition of this sharpened fifth (or flattened sixth). He frequently writes in the major scale with sharpened fourth (i.e., the Lydian mode), e.g., in the polonaise in "Boris." Varlaam's "By the Walls of Kazan" song is in F sharp minor with a flattened second. And these tonal peculiarities all affect Mussorgsky's harmony as, in our own day, the tonal peculiarities of Hungarian folk-music have affected Bartók's.

Victor Belaiev in his "thematic and theoretical analysis" of "Boris"* points, as an example of this, to the harmonic basis of the trumpet fanfare that rings out on Shuisky's first appearance in the coronation scene: four major triads on the descending bass, E, C, A, E. (The same progression recurs later in the scene, where the people cry "Long life and power to you our father!") The key, he says, is C major; the G sharps in the first and last chords are just normal Mussorgskian sharpened fifths; the C sharp in the penultimate chord is an enharmonically written flattened supertonic. This particular instance seems to me very far-fetched. It is much more likely that Mussorgsky, indulging in the characteristic Russian love of harmonic curiosities, was simply playing with a progression of major triads in which the note E should be successively root, third, fifth and root. Nevertheless, although this particular illustration is wrong, the general pro-

---

* Published in the volume, "Boris Godunov: Statii i issledovaniya" (Moscow, 1930).

position it is intended to illustrate is true. There must be dozens of instances in "Boris" alone of Mussorgsky's free use of the major triad on the mediant without any suggestion of modulation.

Compared with Mussorgsky's harmony Borodin's is more or less conventional. Like Balakirev he merely continues the Glinka tradition. The curious progression of third inversions of dominant sevenths all hinging on the note D in the eclipse music of "Prince Igor" was obviously suggested by the passage in "Ruslan" (Lyudmila's abduction) to which I have drawn attention above. Similar progressions of unrelated chords pivoting on a single note common to all are frequent in Russian music. It remained for Rimsky-Korsakov to play on the switchback of a pair of unrelated chords—dominant sevenths a minor third apart—with two notes in common (second movement of "Scheherazade"). Sometimes Borodin follows Glinka even in the weak chromatic slithering of his parts. It is hardly necessary to say that his harmony is full of sharpened fifths and flattened sixths. But one or two points in his music become much more comprehensible when considered in the light of the tonal characteristics we have observed in Mussorgsky. Take, for instance, the opening of the B minor Symphony:

If this is B minor, one is inclined to say, it is B minor only in the Pickwickian sense. But forget for a moment that it is supposed to be B minor, assume for the sake of argument that it is D major, and everything becomes clear at once. The chromatic alterations are the very ones that we find frequently in Mussorgsky: flattened seventh (C natural), flattened second (D sharp for E flat), and the intermediate note between the fifth and sixth degrees of the scale (B flat). It is just as arguable that Ex. 86 is in Mussorgskian D major as that it is in Pickwickian B minor. But, as we have already seen, a tendency to confuse relative major and minor was common in Russian music at this period, and the truth seems to be that Borodin was thinking in a B minor strongly influenced by the tonal peculiarities of the Russian relative major. The important point is that all these chromatic alterations, alike in Borodin and in Mussorgsky, are purely musical in origin—springing either from the modes of Russian folk music or from sensitiveness to the minor flavour of the sharpened fifth (flattened sixth) in the major scale—and have little in common with Wagner's chromatic alterations, which are usually either essentially expressive or else appear in the form of appoggiaturas or passing notes.

Borodin also shows an affinity with Mussorgsky in his free use of unresolved consecutive seconds. I have referred above to Mussorgsky's minor seconds in "Marriage"; the most striking example in Borodin is the accompaniment to his song, "The Sleeping Princess," pervaded throughout by the quiet syncopated throbbing of unresolved seconds —a purely impressionistic effect.* One passage in the song, where these seconds are combined with a descending whole-tone scale, is harmonically one of the most curious Borodin ever wrote. "The Sleeping Princess" was written in 1867, the year before "Marriage," but it is useless to search the Russian music of the next thirty or forty years for traces of the influence of such procedures as these consecutive seconds. For those we must look in French music: Debussy's song, "Le Jet d'Eau" (about 1888) and later works, even d'Indy (e.g., Guilhen's "Au nom du soleil" in "Fervaal"). By the time these things reappeared in Russian music (Stravinsky and his contemporaries) they were the common property of all European composers.† Indeed, in the course of the 1870's, Russian music in general began to fall more and more into line with that of Western Europe, retaining its folk-songish flavour but losing its former spirit of bold experiment. This is particularly true of Russian harmony. From the harmonic point of view Tchaïkovsky and the later, self-trained Rimsky-Korsakov are much less interesting than Glinka and the

---

* See Ex. 61.

† There is a brief, passing effect of seconds, used impressionistically, in Wagner's song, "Im Treibhaus" (1857), but this cannot be compared in either boldness or scope with the Borodin and Mussorgsky examples.

Balakirev circle. Tchaïkovsky's harmony was never the most remarkable feature of his music, though it is worth noting in passing that he, too, sometimes writes flattened sevenths in the major mode (cf. the reapers' dance in the first act of "Onegin"), sharpened fifths and so on, like any Glinka or Mussorgsky. Similarly, the later Rimsky-Korsakov is harmonically interesting only for his reconciliation of the Lisztian-Wagnerian chromatic system with the Russian, a hybrid afterwards still further complicated by Stravinsky, who crossed it with a strain of Debussyism.

Definitely Lisztian traits are perceptible in Russian music as early as the mid-1860's, but probably the first extensive use of quasi-Western chromaticism occurs in the opening of the third act of "May Night," where Rimsky-Korsakov employs progressions of chromatic chords of the seventh and ninth to suggest the magic of a moonlight night. But it is interesting to note how Russian tonal peculiarities are still blended with the chromaticism of what was then "the music of the future." Take this short passage from Rimsky-Korsakov's symphonic picture, "Sadko"* (Ex. 87).

The first, third, fifth and seventh chords contrive to be three things at the same time: *(a)* Lisztian diminished triads or inversions (three of them segments

---
* Composed in 1867 but re-orchestrated, and possibly harmonically revised, in 1891.

87

of the same diminished seventh), *(b)* collections of appoggiaturas (and in all but one case, chromatic appoggiaturas), *(c)* chords in which the only "altered" notes are our old friends the flattened seventh, flattened second and flattened sixth. This reconciliation of definitely Russian tonal instincts with normal chromaticism persisted in Rimsky-Korsakov's work to the end. The following passage from "The Golden Cockerel," his last work (and, except "Kashchey," his most chromatic work), is thoroughly typical:

88   8ves

The flattened B in the first bar looks like a typical Wagnerian "alteration," but it is obvious that it was also sanctioned (shall we put it?) by the Russian sense for the flattened second. And it is noteworthy that the otherwise regular semitonal descent of the bass is interrupted purely for the sake of throwing the characteristic colour of the flattened sixth on the down beat. (It is, of course, quite unnecessary and quite wrong to explain this passage by any theory of passing modulations.) Like all the other nineteenth-century ideas that widened the limits of tonality, these adventures infected the tonal sense with a nearly mortal sickness. Ex. 88 is certainly in A major, just as any passage in "Tristan" can be shown to be in some key or other. But if this is A major, had not the term "A major" lost much of its meaning for Rimsky-Korsakov by that time?

The logical next step was taken by Stravinsky. Even in "The Firebird" (1910) there are many long passages that can, it is true, be related to a tonic but in which one no longer perceives any sense of tonal functions (Debussy had half killed that for Stravinsky). Stravinsky continues in this score to play with the piquant sensuous sound-effects of Rimsky-Korsakov's "Golden Cockerel" harmonies, but here and there he cuts the painter as his master never did. Where he remains diatonic (e.g., in the Berceuse) he is often astonishingly sensitive to the older Russian tonal characteristics. But, as Edwin Evans has shown in his "Musical Pilgrim" analysis of "The Firebird," the thematic germ of the whole work is the interval of the augmented fourth, a dangerous implement of tonal sabotage. With this weakening of the tonal sense in general the special pull of specifically Russian tonal feelings necessarily lost its force and, although the harmony of Stravinsky and other modern Russian composers (particularly contemporary Soviet composers, who remain definitely tonal) owes something to the methods of their predecessors, it is hardly possible to speak any longer of specifically "Russian" harmony.

INDEX.

Agate, Edward, 170, 174.
Alyabiev, 5, 257.
Araja, 2.
—— "Cephalos and Procris," 2.
Arensky, 234, 236.
Ariosto, 22.
Aristotle, 30.
Ayvazovsky, 24.

Bach, 135, 192.
Bakhturin, 27.
Balakirev, 21, 38, 44, 54, 68, 72-9, 82-3, 86-7, 89, 102, 113, 118, 120, 148, 172, 179-215, 219, 235, 237, 242, 246-9, 253-4, 261-2, 268, 271.
—— "Islamey," 36, 73-4, 77, 79, 89, 179, 213.
—— "King Lear," 193-204, 261.
—— Overture on Three Russian Themes, 180, 197, 261.
—— Piano Concerto, 180, 206.
—— Piano Sonata, 180, 205-15.
—— "Russia," 21, 261.
—— Symphony No. 1, 74, 180-91.
—— Symphony No. 2, 180, 186, 189-92, 206.
—— "Tamara," 36, 75, 77-8, 120, 179-80, 186-7, 213.
Baring, Maurice, 152.
Bartók, 267.
Basili, Francesco, 257.
Bax, 205.
Beethoven, 44, 82, 180-2, 194, 199, 257.
Belaïev, M. P., 111, 126, 164, 170, 236, 238.

Belaïev, Victor, 267.
Bellini, 255, 257.
Belsky, V. I., 126.
Berezovsky, 3.
—— "Demofonte," 3.
Berlioz, 55, 89, 106, 198-200, 204.
Bernard, 219.
Bessel, 169, 220-1, 223.
Bizet, 74, 125.
Borodin, 21, 31-2, 34, 37, 58-60, 63, 66-9, 72, 74-5, 79-80, 82, 87-8, 91-4, 106-11, 114, 147-79, 186, 214, 235-6, 240, 251, 268-70.
—— "Arabian Melody," 174.
—— "Aus meinen Tränen," 169, 174-5, 177.
—— "Bogatïrs," 148.
—— "For the shores of thy far native land," 174.
—— "In Central Asia," 80, 88, 162.
—— "Master Pride," 174.
—— "Mlada," 68, 91-4, 106-11, 156-7, 163-4.
—— "Prince Igor," 18, 21, 31, 41, 79, 108-11, 147-68, 172-3, 177, 268.
—— "Rich and Poor," 174.
—— "Sea," 170, 172-3, 175.
—— "Sea Princess," 169-70.
—— "Sleeping Princess," 66, 170, 172, 175-6, 270.
—— "Song of the Dark Forest," 169-71, 175, 177-8.
—— String Quartet, No. 1, 159, 173.
—— String Quartet, No. 2, 80, 162.

Borodin, Symphony No. 1, 80, 148, 170, 236.
—— Symphony No. 2, 21, 34, 63, 66, 69, 148, 155-6, 158, 172-3, 177, 186, 251, 268-9.
—— Symphony No. 3, 160.
—— "Tsar's Bride," 148, 155.
—— "Vergiftet sind meine Lieder," 170, 172, 176-7.
—— "Wondrous Garden," 169, 175.
Bortnyansky, 3.
—— "Creonte," 3.
Brahms, 182, 186, 213, 235.
Braudo, E. M., 149.
Browne, Sir Thomas, 143.
Browning, 136.
Byron, 126, 194.

Calvocoressi, 4, 20, 31, 106, 124.
Canobbio, 3-4.
—— "Reign of Oleg," 4.
Catherine the Great, 3.
Cavos, 5, 13.
—— "Ivan Susanin," 5.
Chaadaev, 252.
Chaliapin, 53.
Chappell, William, 193, 196.
Cherepnin, N. N., 220-3.
Chernov, K., 188.
Cherubini, 257.
Chester, 170.
Chopin, 56, 118, 192, 256.
Christianovich, 74.
Clementi, 56.
Cui, 6, 52, 59, 82, 87, 91-9, 220.
—— "Angelo," 93.
—— "Mlada," 91-9.

Dargomïzhsky, 43-61, 68, 95-6, 123, 125, 252-3, 257, 262-3, 266.
—— "Baba Yaga," 53-4, 57-8.
—— "Esmeralda," 48.
—— "Fantasia on Finnish Themes," 53-4, 58-61, 266.
—— "Kazachok," 52-6.
—— "Rogdana," 47, 54.
—— "Rusalka," 46-51, 53-4.

Dargomïzhsky, "Stone Guest," 43, 48-9, 51, 53, 68, 168, 262-3, 265.
—— "Titular Councillor," 59.
—— "Triumph of Bacchus," 48.
—— "Worm," 59.
David, Ferdinand, 24.
Debussy, 62, 64, 200, 270-1, 273.
Dehn, Siegfried, 7, 45, 257.
Delius, 203.
Dickens, 183.
Didelot, 21.
Donizetti, 147, 255, 257.
Dostoevsky, 22-3, 251, 254.
Dvořák, 207.
Dyaghilev, 138.
Dyanin, Alexander, 154.
—— S. A., 154, 163.

Elgar, 143.
Evans, Edwin, 273.

Famintsyn, 111.
Findeisen, 4, 46, 48-9, 57, 59, 169, 171.
Fomin, 2-4, 15.
—— "Anyuta," 2.
—— "Miller," 4.

Gedeonov, A. M., 11, 29.
—— M. A., 29-30.
—— S. A., 91-3, 97, 99, 106-7, 112.
Glazunov, 163-8, 234-42.
—— Symphony No. 1, 235, 237-8.
—— Other works, 239-41.
Glinka, 1-55, 63, 66, 68, 72, 75-6, 78, 82-3, 89-90, 102, 114, 123, 148, 179, 192, 237, 242, 253, 256-63, 265-6, 268, 270-1.
—— "Capriccio on Russian Themes," 38.
—— "Kamarinskaya," 35, 55, 102, 260-1.
—— "Life for the Tsar," 1-20, 30, 41, 44-6, 48, 51, 258-9, 266.

Index.

Glinka, "Prince Kholmsky," 28, 45.
—— "Ruslan and Lyudmila," 2, 16, 20-42, 45, 47-9, 51, 53, 63, 68, 75, 90, 158, 257, 259, 261, 268.
—— "Valse-Fantaisie," 45.
Goddard, Scott, 69.
Gogol, 56, 216-8, 221-2, 245-9, 253-4, 263.
Golenishchev-Kutuzov, 219.
Goncharov, 244.

Hadden, Cuthbert, 72.
Hadow, Sir Henry, 169.
Haydn, 56.
Heine, 170, 174.
Helena Pavlovna, Grand Duchess, 112.
Herke, Anton, 83.
Hunfalvy, 153.

d'Indy, 270.

Joachim, 186.
Jurgenson, 170, 177.

Karatïgin, V. G., 220.
Karmalina, Lyubov, 157-8, 217-8.
Kashkin, 226-7, 232.
Kastrioto-Skanderbek, Prince, 45.
Kazhinsky, 198.
Khozrev Mirza, 24.
Khubov, 170.
Krïlov, V. A., 91, 94, 106.
Kukolnik, N. V., 13, 26-30, 44, 54.
Kussevitsky, 239.

Laloy, Louis, 220.
Lambert, Constant, 41, 61.
Lamm, Paul, 219-20.
Laroche, 81, 84, 176.
Lavrin, Janko, 254.
Lavrovskaya, 226.
Lenau, 87.
Liszt, 21, 39, 56, 58, 81-90, 103, 106, 114, 118, 182, 205-6, 208, 240, 256, 271.
Litolff, 82.

Lomakin, 83.
Lyadov, A. K., 57, 94, 110, 113, 142, 162, 220, 222, 236.
Lyapunov, 206.

Markovich, N. A., 25-6, 30.
Marschner, 255.
Martin y Soler, 3.
Matinsky, 3-4, 15.
—— "Bazaar at St. Petersburg," 4.
Mayer, Charles, 12-3.
von Meck, Nadezhda, 82, 226.
Méhul, 257.
Melgunov, 256.
Mendelssohn, 44, 195, 200, 235.
Mengden, 84.
de Mercy Argenteau, Comtesse, 175.
Mey, 148.
Meyerbeer, 82.
Milyukova, Antonina (afterwards Tchaïkovskaya), 225, 227-31.
Minkus, 92, 97, 99.
Mirsky, Prince D. S., 21-2.
Molas, Alexandra, 171-2, 217.
Montagu-Nathan, 206.
Mozart, 190, 207, 209, 257.
Mussorgsky, 21, 52-3, 56-8, 61, 69, 72, 75-6, 82-4, 88, 91-4, 99-102, 105, 109, 111-2, 114, 117, 119, 125, 132, 135, 169-70, 173-4, 178-9, 191-2, 215-24, 235, 251-3, 257, 262-71.
—— "Boris Godunov," 18, 52, 61, 69-70, 92, 100, 117, 132, 168, 191, 217, 222-4, 264-8.
—— "Child's Song," 222.
—— "Fair of Sorochintsy," 88, 101, 106, 216-24.
—— "Intermezzo in modo classico," 135.
—— "Khovanshchina," 21, 75, 132, 168, 217-9.
—— "Marriage," 52, 216, 263-4, 269-70.
—— "Mlada," 76, 91-4, 99-102, 105-6, 119, 218, 222.

Mussorgsky, "Night on the Bare Mountain," 53, 58, 84, 105-6, 216, 218, 222-3.
—— "Nursery," 171.
—— "Œdipus," 101.
—— "On the Don," 221.
—— "Peepshow," 111-2.
—— "Pictures from an Exhibition," 132, 215.
—— "Ragamuffin," 171.
—— "Salammbô," 101, 223.
—— "Taking of Kars," 76, 102.

Napoleon III, 175.
Napravnik, 231.
Nekrassov, 174.
Newman, Ernest, 90, 210.
Newmarch, Rosa, 170, 206.
Nicholas I, 13.

Odoevsky, Prince, 9, 12, 48.
Ossovsky, 234.

Paesiello, 5.
Pashkevich, 3-4.
Petrov, O. A., 11, 13, 24, 218-9, 221.
Puccini, 74, 255.
Purgold, Alexandra (see Molas).
—— Nadezhda (afterwards Rimskaya-Korsakova),216-7.
Pushkin, 21-6, 30, 124-8, 174, 226-7.

Ralston, W. R. S., 57.
von Riesemann, 92-3.
Rimsky-Korsakov, A. N., 104.
—— A. Y., 25.
—— N. A., 4, 18, 31, 34-5, 38-41, 50, 52-4, 56-7, 64, 66-70, 72-4, 76-9, 82-7, 89, 107, 112-42, 148, 161-8, 171, 179-81, 185, 187-8, 190-2, 198, 214, 216, 219, 221-2, 235-8, 240, 244, 247-51, 253, 255-6, 262-5, 268, 270-3.
—— "Antar," 73-4, 77-8, 86, 119, 262.
—— "Christmas Eve," 18, 35, 70, 90, 118, 121, 125, 191, 221.

Rimsky-Korsakov, N. A., "Easter Overture," 114.
—— "Fantasia on Serbian Themes," 77, 119.
—— "Golden Cockerel," 36, 40, 53, 78-9, 115, 120, 125, 131, 251, 272-3.
—— "Kashchey," 125, 272.
—— "Kitezh," 42, 79, 115, 125-7, 129, 132, 251.
—— "Maid of Pskov" (see "Pskovityanka").
—— "May Night," 35, 68, 103-4, 114, 271.
—— "Mlada" (1872), 91-4, 99-105.
—— "Mlada" (1890), 36, 73, 77, 94-9, 101, 103-4, 106-7, 113-21, 125, 134, 250.
—— "Mozart and Salieri," 53, 125.
—— "Pan Voevoda," 125.
—— "Pskovityanka," 4, 52, 92, 113, 132, 262.
—— "Sadko" (opera), 77-8, 115, 117-9, 123, 125, 127, 129, 250.
—— "Sadko" (symphonic poem), 34, 51, 78, 85-6, 262, 271-2.
—— "Scheherazade," 36, 63, 66-7, 69, 77-9, 114, 119, 133, 138-43, 164, 268.
—— "Servilia," 123, 125.
—— "Skazka," 35.
—— "Snegurochka" ("Snow Maiden"), 31, 39, 41, 89, 104-5, 114, 118, 125.
—— "Spanish Capriccio," 114.
—— String Quartet in F, 99.
—— "Tsar Saltan," 31, 38, 115, 121-37, 250.
—— "Tsar's Bride," 18, 38, 123, 125, 127, 148.
—— "Vera Sheloga," 125.
Röder, 238.
Rossini, 35, 147.
Rubinstein, Anton, 83.

Sakhnovsky, 220.
Salvador-Daniel, 74.
Sarti, 4.

Index.

Schönberg, 64.
Schubert, 33, 54, 260.
Schumann, 82, 174, 177, 199, 235.
Serov, 16, 82, 111.
Shakespeare, 194-8, 200.
Shakhovsky, Prince, 24.
Shebalin, 219-20.
Shestakova, Lyudmila, 46, 148.
Shilovsky, 227, 230-1.
Shirkov, V. F., 26-30.
Shonorov, V. A., 156.
Shterich, 24.
Sibelius, 60, 190.
Skryabin, 71, 213-4.
—— "Poem of Ecstasy," 71.
—— "Prometheus," 71.
Sokolov, V. T., 45, 49.
Spencer, Herbert, 250.
Spinoza, 250.
Spohr, 255.
Sreznevsky, 93.
Stassov, V. V., 86, 91-2, 106, 108-9, 148-9, 152, 154-8, 160, 164, 171-4, 193-4, 196, 198, 202, 217, 219, 246, 270.
Stepanov, P. A., 46.
Strauss, Richard, 255.
Stravinsky, 34, 39, 53, 70, 251, 266, 271, 273-4.
—— "Firebird," 34, 36, 39, 41, 53, 70, 273.
—— "Rite of Spring," 41, 266.

Taneev, S. I., 163.
Tarnovsky, 25.
Tausig, 87.
Tchaïkovsky, A. I., 231.
—— M. I., 144-5, 225-6.
—— P. I., 15, 18-9, 39, 52, 76-7, 81-3, 95, 102, 136, 143-6, 171, 176, 178, 186, 191-2, 194, 198, 200, 207, 225-34, 236, 255, 265, 270-1.
—— Andante and Finale, Op. 79, 146.
—— "Dread Minute," 171.
—— "Eugene Onegin," 226-33, 271.

Tchaïkovsky, "Nutcracker," 39, 52.
—— "Oprichnik," 136.
—— Overture, "1812," 76.
—— Piano Concerto No. 3, Op. 75, 146.
—— "Romeo and Juliet," 194.
—— Serenade for Strings, 102.
—— Suite No. 2, 52.
—— Suite No. 3, 191.
—— Symphony No. 2, 52.
—— Symphony No. 3, 191.
—— Symphony No. 4, 15, 186, 231-2.
—— Symphony No. 5, 18-9, 207.
—— Symphony No. 6 ("Pathétique"), 143-6.
—— "Tempest," 194.
Titov, Alexey, 5.
—— Sergey, 5.
Tolstoy, Alexey, 174.
—— Leo, 244, 246-9, 251.
—— Theophil, 111.

Ulibishev, A. D., 190.

Varlamov, 257.
Verdi, 200, 255.
Verstovsky, 5, 260.
Vielhorsky, Count, 11.
Volkov, 2.
Vorobieva, 13, 24.

Wagner, 16, 82, 114-5, 117-8, 123, 125, 129, 133-4, 147, 171, 235, 253, 255-6, 265, 269-72.
Weber, 16, 21, 31, 38-9, 50, 74.
Wilde, Oscar, 241.

Yastrebtsev, 85, 87, 98, 105, 108, 140-2.
Yusupov, Prince, 11.

Zaremba, 111.
Zhukovsky, 8, 23, 246.
Zinin, 170.